CHINA FOR AMERICA

Export Porcelain of the 18th and 19th Centuries

Herbert, Peter and Nancy Schiffer

Schiffer Publishing Ltd

Box E, Exton, Pennsylvania 19341

Library of Congress catalog card number: 80–51594

ISBN: 0-91683823-4

Printed in the United States of America

Dedication:

To Homer and Ethel, Jim and Migs

Acknowledgments

Our sincere thanks to the following friends and associates whose interest in this project has helped us to find and identify services for American families. A project of this nature is always a team effort and we thank them for being on our side.

Mrs. Joseph Alsop; Lu D. Bartlett; Lucy Batchelder, Peabody Museum of Salem; Esther Brumberg, Museum of the City of New York; Steven M. Carother; Anne R. Cassidy, New York State Office of Parks and Recreation; Thomas Jefferson Coolidge, Jr.; J. Emlen Woodruff; John Quentin Feller, Professor of History at the University of Scranton and visiting curator of Chinese Export Porcelain at The Peabody Museum of Salem; James Galley; Benjamin and Cora Ginsburg; Elinor Gordon; Robert C. Graham, Sr., Graham Gallery, Ltd.; Barry A. Greenlaw, The Bayou Bend Collection; Robert D. Gries, Lucile and Robert H. Gries Charity Fund; Collier Havens; Gouverneur Morris Helfenstein; Kathryn B. Hiesinger, Philadelphia Museum of Art; Jon Peter Hulleberg; J. Kenneth Jones, The Charleston Museum; Theodore H. Kapnek, Sr.; Robert Keeth; Cynthia Koch, Old Barracks Museum; E. R. Kosche, The Bennington Museum; S. Dean Levy, Bernard and S. Dean Levy, Inc.; Lino Lipinsky, John Jay Homestead State Historic Site; Samuel L. Lowe, Jr.; Patricia A. Mallory, Eastern National Parks and Monument Association; J. Jefferson Miller, Smithsonian Institution; Dr. James E. Mooney, The Historical Society of Pennsylvania; Jeffrey H. Munger, Museum of Fine Arts, Boston; Fred B. Nadler, Antiques; Philip J. Richmond; William R. Sargent, Museum of the American China Trade; Russell Scheider, Antiques; Karol A. Schmiegel, Winterthur Museum; Mrs. Samuel Schwartz; Matthew and Elisabeth Sharpe; Raymond V. Shepherd, Cliveden, National Trust for Historic Preservation; Faye Simkin, The New York Public Library; Philip Smith, Philadelphia Maritime Museum; Mr. and Mrs. Richard M. Stiner; John Barclay Swain, Photographer, Nantucket Historical Association; Phoebe Prime Swain, Nantucket Historical Association; Betty O. Tyson, North Carolina Museum of History; Leroy H. True, Nantucket Historical Association; Linda White; Thomas D. and Constance R. Williams; Carol Wojtowicz, Mutual Assurance Company; Richard Wolfe, Boston Medical Library; Dolores Ziff, Pennsylvania Hospital.

Table of Contents

Acknowledgments   iv

Early Chinese-American Commerce with Porcelain   7

Armorial Decorations   31

Monogrammed Decorations   59

Color Plates   93

Eagle Decorations   109

Masonic and Political Decorations   137

Marine Decorations   153

Western Landscape Decorations   167

Chinese Landscape Decorations   181

Floral Decorations   195

Footnotes   209

Bibliography   214

Index   218

Early Chinese - American commerce with porcelain

The importation of Chinese porcelain to America was only a small part of early Sino-American commercial trade. From the first voyages of American ships to China in 1784, American vessels brought cargoes of varied types and origins dominated by tea, silk, and a coarse cotton fabric known as nankeen. But even before American ships went to China, porcelain was made for and used in America.

The earliest examples of Chinese porcelain known to have been made for Americans were intended for Spanish colonists living in present-day Mexico and Spanish California. American Indians at Drake's Bay, north of San Francisco, acquired Chinese ceramics from a ship-wrecked Spanish galleon. Wares excavated at the Drake's Bay Indian sites were mainly blue and white, a type which has been identified as Ming dynasty ware of the period circa 1585. This type of decoration had dominated Chinese export porcelain up to the Ming period and would dominate the American market thereafter. This ware was distinguished by a transparent glaze covering underglaze, cobalt-blue designs typical of the Chinese Ming period. Motifs on the thin, white ceramic included spotted deer, cranes, peacocks, phoenixes, butterflies and dragonflies, flora, ponds, rocks and clouds.

Spanish traders in Mexico imported not only blue-and-white, but shards also

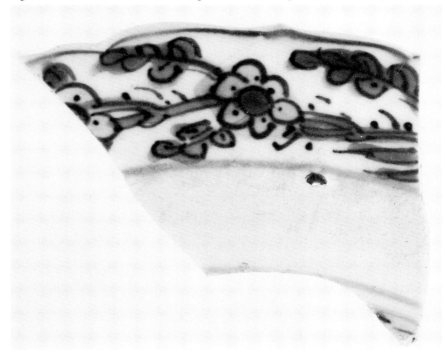

Small thin white porcelain fragment with underglaze blue decoration. Excavated at Drake's Bay, California in 1940. Identified as Ming dynasty ware, circa 1585. *(Courtesy: Lowie Museum of Anthropology, University of California, Berkeley)*

Another fragment excavated at Drake's Bay, California, this is a portion of the inside bottom of a small plate with foot rim, circa 1585. *(Courtesy: Lowie Museum of Anthropology, University of California, Berkeley)*

have been found of a thick, coarse stoneware, suggesting wine or water jars of Chinese or Indo-Chinese origin, which may have been carried by the galleon[?]

From 1585 through 1784, forms and decor of porcelain from East Coast sites resembled those found on the West Coast. Eastern homes were often furnished with Oriental wares. For example, a 1760 Williamsburg, Virginia inventory listed a Chinese export tea pot and stand, slop basin, tea cannister, cups, saucers and coffee pot. Excavations at Williamsburg's Wetherburn Tavern have disclosed a bowl decorated in underglaze blue in a 1750–75 context[3]

Additional shards of blue-and-white porcelain from eighteenth century sites have been excavated in the "Society Hill" and "Penn's Landing" sections of Philadelphia[4] and similar sites from Charleston, South Carolina to Louisburg, Canada. Other searches of Virginia and Pennsylvania sites also have disclosed porcelain with elaborate polychrome decoration, yet these shards were not nearly as common as the blue-and-white.

Determining exactly when porcelain sets were brought to America is clouded because the term "China" as a reference to ceramics was used in the vaguest way in historical documents of the early periods. No distinction was made between genuine Chinese porcelain and imitation European wares. Benjamin Franklin, for example, first referred to the appearance of "China" in his house about 1730, but it is unclear from his reference whether he meant genuine porcelain from China or imitation[5]

America was also beginning to produce porcelain wares of its own in the late eighteenth century. By 1769, kaolin had been located along the bed of White Clay Creek, south of Philadelphia. The Bonnin and Morris China Manufactory was opened by Gousse Bonnin and Anthony Morris in Philadelphia which managed to produce a number of fine quality porcelain wares, the first in America, before it succumbed to bankruptcy in 1772.

Merchants of British North America were not permitted, under the terms of the 1651 Navigation Act and subsequent legislation, to sail in their own ships to East Asia; rather, they were obliged to purchase Chinese goods on the London market, where the goods were deposited by the British East India Company. Such

8

a system was intended to guarantee the British a continuous influx of wealth from the colonies. These acts required from the colonial merchant the payment of middleman profits which he would not have had to pay had he been able to sail directly to China. From 1750 on, Colonial American merchants had the mercantile and navigational expertise, and the necessary capital, to embark on such direct voyages themselves.

In 1751, 1753, and 1754, Benjamin Franklin and William Allen sent their ship *Argo* on three separate missions in search of a direct Northwest Passage route to China. These unsuccessful voyages angered British authorities who questioned the propriety of the colonial ventures. Had such a route been opened by the colonials, and commerce initiated, violation of practically every Navigation Act would have been committed. The disputes were only laid to rest when the *Argo* returned to Philadelphia in 1754, at the end of its third and final attempt, having neither located a Northwest Passage to China nor established a Labrador trade. It would be another thirty years before American merchants would again seriously entertain the prospect of direct trade with China.[6]

British Captain James Cook, on his 1776 Pacific venture, attempted to locate a Northwest Passage to China by sailing up the Pacific coast of North America. The voyage was followed with keen interest in early America particularly by Benjamin Franklin. While the voyage was in progress, Franklin secured a military order forbidding American naval interference with Cook's ship because of its extraordinary navigational and commercial importance. Among reports of the voyage that reached America by the early 1780's were Lieutenant John Rickman's account, published in London in 1781 and in Philadelphia in 1783, and Seaman John Ledyard's account, printed in Hartford in the same year. Two vital points emerged from these accounts. First, the Northwest Passage had not been found from the Pacific side. If Oriental commerce was to be pursued, the traditional routes around Cape Horn and the Cape of Good Hope would have to be utilized. Secondly, fur pelts secured from Indians of the Northwest Coast for practically no money, fetched extraordinary prices from Chinese merchants in Canton. A profitable trade might be undertaken shipping these goods across the Pacific, and taking on Chinese goods for Western markets.[7]

John Ledyard of Connecticut was one of the few Americans aboard Cook's ship. On his return to the United States in 1783, he contacted the major merchants of the United States in an attempt to find underwriters for a Pacific Northwest fur voyage. In May of 1783, Robert Morris of Philadelphia took an interest in his scheme. Morris had a propensity for unconventional business practices and was sadly aware of the ongoing uncertainties in the new nation's traditional Atlantic and Caribbean commerce. However, in Morris's efforts to secure other underwriters to share the risk of such a voyage, he ran into difficulties because of the equally great uncertainty of Northwest Coast navigation. A partnership was finally struck between Robert Morris and William Duer of Philadelphia, and Daniel Parker and John Holker of New York, with joint capitalization of $120,000. Their intended ship was to carry ginseng as its main cargo, along with coinage and locally secured furs which avoided the need for a Northwest Coast passage.

The choice of ginseng in the cargo was determined from highly successful trade of this herb with the Chinese through England. Previously, the Dutch, at Albany, had traded "hardware, trinkets, and rum" to the Indians for ginseng that grew on the hills near Stockbridge, Massachusetts. The roots were bundled, shipped down the Hudson River, and on to Amsterdam and London. They were sold to the British East India Company at a profit of five hundred percent. The ginseng was then resold profitably in China by the British. The Chinese valued this herb highly as an aphrodisiac. In December, 1783, the sloop *Harriet* of Boston set out for China with a large cargo of ginseng. The ship, however, did not reach China on this voyage. When the *Harriet* rounded the Cape of Good Hope with this precious cargo, it ran into a British East India Company ship, whose captain was so startled at the possibility of American trade with China that he traded double its weight in tea for the *Harriet's* ginseng.[8]

Elaborate preparations were made for Robert Morris and company's planned voyage. A three hundred and sixty ton Baltimore-built vessel was christened the *Empress of China*. In New York, a cargo was loaded consisting of thirty tons of Appalachian ginseng, 2,600 furs, and the remainder of the freight in money, pig lead and woolen cloth. Revolutionary War expertise was drawn upon in the selection of the captain, John Green of Philadelphia, recently relieved of naval duties, and the business agent or supercargo Samuel Shaw, recently aide-de-camp of General Henry Knox. Shaw was also U. S. consul designate to China and foresaw a vast market in China for American ginseng. Shaw wrote to Secretary of State John Jay:

> The otherwise useless produce ginseng of (America's) mountains and forests will, in a considerable degree, supply her with this luxury (tea). The Europeans have seen, the first year, a single ship, not one fifth part of whose funds consisted of ready money, procure a cargo for the same articles and on equally good terms, as those of their own terms. It is probable that there will always be a sufficient demand for the article to make it equally valuable?[9]

Robert Morris wrote Jay that he was "sending some ships to China in order to encourage others in the adventurous pursuit of commerce![10]

Morris remained in Philadelphia to plan additional voyages and manage his other enterprises. As a final preparation, the ship's departure from New York was arranged for Washington's Birthday, February 22, 1784.

The trading conditions which the first United States ship encountered in China were unlike any that Americans were accustomed to in any other port of the world.

In the mid-eighteenth century, Chinese foreign trade merchants at Canton formed an association which won official government sanction only after paying heavy bribes to the Imperial Court. It took the name *kung-hang,* "officially authorized guild." Westerners came to refer to this organization by its pidgin English title, "cohong," and its members as "hong" merchants. In 1784, this was the only Chinese trading organization Western seafarers could trade with. Each would accept payment in coinage and ginseng, furs and rice (which could be imported duty-free).

The cohong would willingly trade with ships of any Western nation, so long as duties were paid and the "eight regulations" were met. Under these "regulations," no contraband could be introduced, and most important, no contact could be made with Chinese other than members of the cohong and the Customs Service. The regulations read in part: " 'foreign barbarians' may not leave the factories except on the 8th, 18th and 28th days of the moon, when they may take the air in the company of a Linguist to visit the Flower Gardens and the Hinam joss house but not in droves of over ten at one time; that foreigners must deal only with the hong merchants and must not sell to rascally nations goods subject to duty, that these may smuggle them and thereby defraud his Celestial Majesty's revenue, and that neither women, guns, spears nor arms of any kind can be brought to the factories."[11] The Canton trade was carried out wholly without the sanction of diplomacy. There were no official relations between China and any Western states except Russia, which engaged in an overland treaty-regulated trade with China and rarely sent ships to Canton.[12]

These conditions were largely unknown to the promoters of the *Empress* voyage. Morris was unaware, for example, of the Chinese willingness to trade with all comers and was under the mistaken impression that a foreign vessel would be permitted to trade only after its captain had produced a suitable letter of introduction from the foreign government. Therefore, Captain Green had acquired such a document from Charles Thomson, then Secretary of the Congress. In spite of these unknowns, the vast quanity of ginseng which the *Empress* brought secured it an immediate and hospitable reception in Canton. Thomas Randal, the assistant supercargo, wrote that the *Empress* unloaded "the largest quanity of ginseng ever brought to the Chinese market, more than all the British and Portuguese ships had brought for the year 1784."[13]

A return cargo was then taken on for the home market. The bulk of the return freight consisted of teas: souchong, bohea, hyson, gunpowder and hyson skin. Other general sale items included six hundred silk women's gloves, silk yard goods, cotton fabrics including nankeen cloth, and Chinese cinnamon and porcelain. Among the more unusual items in the cargo was an entire set of home furnishings crafted by Canton artisans for Robert Morris. The order included over one hundred dollars worth of hand-painted wall paper and paper borders; four lacquered fans and a dressing box for Mrs. Morris; a glass specially decorated for that box by one "Puqua, painter on glass"; a case of porcelain; and bundle of mounted silk window blinds with bamboo ribs. This shipment to Morris represents the largest single order of Chinese household furnishings ever placed by an American up to the time. Among the items on the return voyage was a porcelain bowl bearing the words "*Empress of China,* Captain John Green" and a stylized drawing of a ship (see pages 154—5.) The portrait was not of the ship itself, but a copy of an available etching *Hall* from the frontispiece of William A. Hutchinson's *A Treatise on Practical Seamanship* published in 1777 and 1791 in Liverpool. The "*Empress of China* bowl" was apparently the first custom made porcelain for the United States market. Like the *Grand Turk* bowl which is fully documented (see pages 154—5), this bowl was possibly the gift of a Chinese merchant to Captain Green.

The *Empress of China* arrived in New York in May, 1785. The boat's general sale items were disposed of, netting the owners a profit of $30,000, a twenty-five percent gain on their original investment. While this percentage was not high relative to subsequent China trade voyages, especially those from New England, it was nevertheless a precedent-setting voyage in that a new water route had proved profitable, and the commercial mechanisms in Canton viable.

Newspaper accounts of the *Empress'* return appeared up and down the East Coast almost immediately. In what was perhaps a typical American newspaper exultation on the commercial significance of Morris' venture, Boston's <u>Massachusetts Centinel</u> of May 18, 1785, editorialized that "this passage is one of the greatest in nautical prodigies we ever recollect hearing.[14] Philadelphia's <u>Pennsylvania Packet</u>, of May 16, 1785, made the slightly more subdued observation that Americans would no longer have to import Chinese goods via Europe:

> As the ship has returned with a
> full cargo, and as such articles as we gen-
> erally import from Europe, it presages
> a happy period of our being able to
> dispense with that burdensome traffic
> which we have here to fore carried on
> to the prejudice of our rising empire. [15]

The *Empress of China* was quickly readied for a return passage to Canton. That second voyage, in addition to being commercially successful in standard China trade items, brought back twenty-four mother-of-pearl mounted fans, one of which may have been the fan bearing what seems to be the only known picture of the *Empress of China*.

The United States government encouraged the China trade by maintaining a favorable tariff policy. Even though individual states had levied a tariff on tea even before the adoption of the Constitution, and Congress passed its first tea tariff in 1789, tea was one of the twenty items that had an import duty.[16]

As Britain made known her toleration of American-Asiatic trade, she also demonstrated hostility toward the traditional American trade with the West Indian colonies, which she wished to reserve for Imperial shipping. After the commencement of Anglo-French hostilities in 1793, neutral American shipping with French West Indian colonies was regularly harassed by Britain. In that year, Britain seized over three hundred American ships which had been trading with the French West Indies. Many American merchants who had made the basis of their fortunes in West Indian shipping (like Robert Morris, E. H. Derby, J. Peabody and Stephen Girard), were reluctant to relinquish this lucrative trade, despite British chastisement. Girard went so far as to furnish his ships with duplicate sets of documents: a genuine set, which revealed trade with French islands; and a spurious set, which showed no such commerce. The 1795 Jay Treaty, after diplomatic and Congressional wrangling, was mute on the key questions of American-West Indian trade and American neutrality rights. The agreement did somewhat stabilize American trade with England, which, as early as 1789, had surpassed all pre-war tonnage levels.[17] However, Britains' tolerance of American trade with the Orient was not sufficient in itself to induce American merchants to embark on their own Asian voyages. The favorable tea tariff, Jay's Treaty, and, more importantly, the fantastic profits of the *Empress* voyages, encouraged other merchants to send out China voyages. A "China fever" took hold. One month after the *Empress's* return, the *United States,* backed

Stephen Girard's *Montesquieu* (above), *Rousseau* and *Desdemona* (below) were frequent visitors to Canton during the first quarter of the nineteenth century. The lower photograph was taken after the ships had been converted for use in whaling hunts. Their top masts have been removed. The copper sheathing is high out of the water indicating that they were not loaded. These were small but capacious ships. Stephen Girard was one of the more important American merchants to China, and these ships were among the most efficient of their time. *(Courtesy: top, J. Goldstein; bottom, Whaling Museum, New Bedford, Massachusetts)*

by friends of Morris, sailed for China and India.[18]   Although it never reached Canton, it was the first American vessel to reach Pondicherry, Acheen in Sumatra, and the Coramandel Coast.[19]

The earliest American ships in the China trade were:

Empress of China (Shaw, captain)	New York February 1784—New York May 1785
Pallas (Randall)	China—Baltimore August 1785
Hope (Shaw)	New York December 1785—New York 1786
Grand Turk	Salem December 1785—Salem January 1787
Empress of China (II)	New York 1786—New York 1787
Experiment	New York 1786—New York 1787
Canton	Philadelphia 1786—Philadelphia 1787
Alliance	Philadelphia 1787—Philadelphia 1788
Asia	Philadelphia 1787—Philadelphia 1788
General Washington	Providence 1787—Providence 1788
Columbia	Boston 1787—Boston 1790
Jay	New York 1788—New York 1789

From 1786 on, commerce with the Orient developed so quickly that other coastal towns joined in the China trade. New Haven, Salem, Boston, Baltimore and Providence each took an active part. At least a dozen China trade firms came into existence in Philadelphia alone. One of them was headed by the mayor himself, Charles Wharton.[20]

On September 30, 1787, the *Columbia* set out from Boston, with the intention of following Ledyard's scheme of bringing Pacific Northwest furs to Canton. When the Columbia returned on August 9, 1790, it was not only the first American ship to utilize Ledyard's scheme, but also the first American ship to go around the world.[21]

Between 1784 and 1804, as many as thirty-one ships per year went from the United States to China. After 1804, until the end of the old China trade in 1846, the number of American voyages leveled off between thirty and forty per year.[22]

Voyages from America to China were usually financed by merchants of established means sending out their own ships on their own account or by investors of smaller means pooling their resources. In both cases, after about 1792, some of the formidable problems of these distant trips were eased when financing was facilitated by insurance companies. While the actual outfitting of the vessel was expensive, the acquisition of large amounts of cash was a particularly vexing problem. Insurance companies eased the process in some cases by lending money to China traders. Large sums were directly advanced for the purchase of gold and silver coinage, which was then exchanged in China for Chinese goods. After the goods were sold in the West, the insurance companies were repaid principal plus interest.[23]

China traders were closely affiliated, both in directorship and in volume of business, with the Insurance Company of North America, the Phoenix Insurance Company (Truxtun and John Latimer, the principles), the Insurance Company of Pennsylvania (Girard), the Atlantic Insurance Company (Ashabel Ralston), and the Franklin Insurance Company (Mordecai Lewis, Tobias Wagner, Thomas I. Wharton, and Charles N. and James A. Bancker). Thomas Pym Cope appears to be the only merchant who permitted his cargoes to go uninsured. Since the China trade frequently involved full war risk premiums, he felt that, with the saving on insurance, he could build more ships than he would lose.

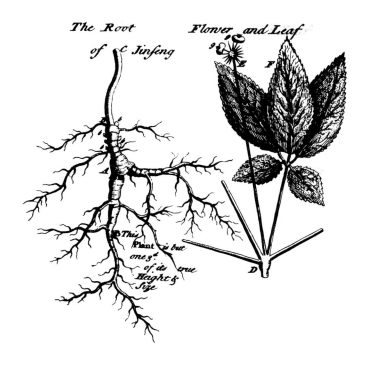

The Root of ye Jinseng

Flower and Leaf

Chinese ginseng plant, original drawing by Father Jean Du Hall De Gartoux, China, 1709. From a <u>Description of China, I</u> *(London: T. Gardner, 1738).*

The persistent problem of choosing cargo for Canton plagued American China traders. Several basic criteria had to be met. The cargo had to be a commodity the Chinese wanted. Any product picked up further than 1,000 miles away from Canton had to be highly valuable relative to its weight and bulk, since much of the sale price would have to offset freight costs. Only products of continously expanding demand and constant high price in Canton could be considered. It was difficult to predict when competitors would arrive in Canton with the same cargo, giving the cohong the opportunity to negotiate the price. The ideal cargo would be readily integrated with American trade to Europe.[24]

It was universally realized in the American mercantile community that profit was best generated through a rapid turnover of cargo, rather than the shipment of static cargoes like ginseng over extended routes. Ginseng, furthermore, was particularly prone to gluts in the Canton market, as soon as China neared its annual consumption ceiling of 2,000 piculs (or $100,000 worth). The drug was not popularly consumed and remained an imperial monopoly item for the duration of the old China trade.

American merchants were aware from contacts in Europe and Asia that as the British consolidated their hold on India in the 1770's they began to ship large quantities of Indian opium to China. The drug was not native to China and for centuries the Chinese had imported it for medicinal purposes. It may also have been used to a growing extent as a narcotic, for the widespread habitual use of the drug seems to have taken hold in China by the mid-eighteenth century, after the introduction of smoking to China from the New World. Smoking opium was a more convenient and leisurely manner of ingesting the drug than eating it, and resulted in an increased popular demand for the preparation.

15

<u>Pavot Somnifere</u>, from a French herbal of about 1888.

In 1800 the Chinese government banned the use and importation of opium, because of the drug's lethal nature if habitually used, its consequent deleterious social effect, and because the favorable balance of trade which China had traditionally enjoyed with the West was rapidly deteriorating. Even though the trade had been declared illegal, Britain was reluctant to relinquish it, and devised an elaborate smuggling system that remained substantially unchanged from 1800 through the 1830's. British ships brought opium from India and weighed anchor in the outer reaches of the Canton estuary, beyond the normal range of patrol of the Chinese Customs Service. Chinese smugglers, known as "shopmen" or "country traders," surreptitiously sailed out to the opium ships, paid in silver for the narcotic, and spirited it ashore. The British ships, loaded with Chinese silver, then sailed on to anchorage and the merchants either invested all the silver in Chinese goods or saved a portion of it for future opium purchases in India.

Perhaps the smoothest aspect of the British system was that the British East India Company, although extensively involved in the sale and cultivation of opium in India, took no part in the actual transshipment of the drug to China, and reiterated this fact when Chinese officials complained and threatened to close down legitimate company trade in Canton. The actual freighting of Indian opium to China was subcontracted to private trade firms such as Jardine, Matheson and Company, Dent and Company, and occasionally, after 1815, to American merchants like Benjamin Chew Wilcocks and John Latimer. The Company used the proceeds it derived indirectly from opium sales to the Chinese for the purchase of its own Chinese goods. From 1800 to 1834, the company purchased about three quarters of all Chinese maritime exports, much of it with opium trade silver.[5]

American merchants observed the smooth operation of the British opium system long before they themselves became involved in the commerce. Their opinions remained essentially unchanged during the period of their participation. Many American merchants came to see opium's "legitimacy" in the same way that the British did. Boston merchant Robert Bennet Forbes reflected that view when he wrote that "dealing opium was not looked upon by the British government, by the East India Company, or by the merchants as a smuggling transaction. It was viewed as a legitimate business as long as the drug was sold on the coast, outside the pro-

Turkish opium plant from <u>Commentarii in VI libros de Medica Materia, II,</u> by Pier Mattioli, *(Venice Apud Felicem Vargrisium, 1583).*

fessed jurisdiction of China." For Forbes, and others, engaging in the opium trade entailed no moral crisis, and was a simple matter of following "the right example of England, the East India Company, the countries that cleared it for China, and the merchants to whom I had always been accustomed to look up to as the exponents of all that was honorable in trade." [26]

Despite Forbes' claims, the opium trade was not, in reality, a legitimate business comparable to the trades in tea, coinage, ginseng, porcelain, and other commodities which Westerners and Chinese traditionally exchanged. Although the drug actually passed from Western hands to Chinese hands offshore, vital processes of the contraband trade did in fact occur in Canton, within the bounds of Chinese jurisdiction. It was in Canton, and not aboard ships offshore, where the operations center of the opium trade was located, where deals were finalized, and where English language circulars regularly listed opium prices. Furthermore, it was in Canton where Western merchants habitually spent specie which they knew had been illegally obtained within China by native smugglers. The Chinese officials had the right, even in terms of Western law, to sequester, if not confiscate, such funds. Perhaps a more candid description of the traffic was offered by Philadelphia merchant John Latimer:

> You are aware that the trade in opium is illegal. The system is perfect. A dealer pays the money down and at the same time receives the order to go to the ship for it. We never see it at all. Foreign merchants reside here constantly who are known to have no other business than the opium and are never mentioned. [27]

Latimer was, variously, the President of the Society of the Cincinnati, the individual who took charge of the illegitimate daughter of another trader who abandoned the child in China, and an outspoken advocate of mercantile ethics in other areas[28]

An even blunter statement of the propriety of the opium trade, indicative of the lack of moral crisis in the minds of smugglers, was offered in 1829 by the second

American consul to Canton, Benjamin Chew Wilcocks. In that year, Wilcocks offered John Whitall the captaincy of the ship *New Jersey* on a China opium voyage. Whitall, although a bonafide captain who had previously been in charge of the *New Jersey* on a non-opium voyage, refused, on moral grounds, to accept Wilcocks' offer to partake in the drug business. Wilcocks was indignant at the moral stance taken by the captain and wrote:

> I almost wished I had not heard his objections to going into our employ, which have lessened him in my opinion. I hope I have due and proper respect for the prejudices of my fellow man, but when a Captain stipulates for the particular articles which he will take on my ship, why let him go *you know where* for a cargo. I have done with him forever.[29]

Moral crisis did not, then, deter early Americans from engaging in this type of enterprise. What did hold back American entrepreneurs was that they lacked a ready source for large quantities of opium. Traditionally, Americans had exported small quantities of opium westward from India for medicinal uses in North America. British authorities were understandably reluctant to let American traders ship large quantities eastward, except when their own shipping was incapacitated, as in 1815 due to Napoleon. By 1804, the Boston firm of J. and T. H. Perkins had advised its supercargoes to keep their eyes open for sources of large quantities of opium.[30]

It was Philadelphia merchants who located an alternate source of opium in Smyrna, Turkey. Americans had been trading in this port under the auspices of the British Levant Company. The British, with a ready source of opium in India, had never taken a serious interest in shipping Smyrna opium around Africa or across the Levant to China. Philadelphia merchants William Waln and R. H. Wilcocks were apparently the first to attempt this operation. Their major informant on the scheme's feasibility may have been William Stewart, a Philadelphian who had been American Consul in Smyrna, and who returned to Philadelphia in late 1803 or early 1804. Waln and Wilcocks dispatched the brig *Pennsylvania* to Smyrna in 1804, with Stewart taking a small interest in the outbound cargo. The supercargoes of the vessel were the owner's kinsmen, Benjamin Chew Wilcocks and his younger brother James.[31] Benjamin later rose to prominence as the American Consul at Canton, a job he held simultaneously with his position as one of that port's pre-eminent opium merchants. Under the supervision of the Wilcocks brothers, the *Pennsylvania* unloaded its cargo of tea, sugar, and spices, and took on fifty chests of Smyrna opium, forty-nine were consigned to the supercargo, and one to the brig's master as private speculation. Also taken aboard were 8,200 Spanish dollars, no doubt because of the experimental nature of the other cargo.

In March, 1805, the ship cleared from Smyrna for Batavia. The opium seems to have gotten as far as Batavia, but it is unclear whether the ship went on from there to Canton, the brothers seem to have been reluctant to take the contraband cargo all the way on the first experimental voyage. They themselves proceeded to Canton, where Benjamin remained. James returned to Philadelphia on the *Pennsylvania* and went back to Canton the following year as supercargo of the

Sylph, bringing more Smyrna opium.

The first recorded arrival of an American opium ship in China occurred in June, 1806, when the Baltimore brig *Eutaw* brought "twenty-six chests, fifty-three boxes" of opium to Canton. The following month the *Sylph* arrived with thirty-three cases. The ship also carried Spanish dollars, indicating that American merchants were not confident enough in opium to send an entire shipload.

Waln and the Wilcocks had demonstrated the feasibility of two opium routes: Smyrna-Batavia and Smyrna-Canton. After 1815, they demonstrated the feasibility of limited opium shipment from India as well. Other firms were quick to follow in their footsteps. Willing and Francis, successor firm to Willing and Morris, may have shipped opium to China as early as 1805 aboard their ship *Bingham.* Stephen Girard and his employees and later competitors, the Wagners and Blights, took an early interest in the pioneer voyages. In January, 1806, Girard wrote his supercargoes: "I am very much in favor of investing heavily in opium. While the war lasts, opium will support a good price in China."[32]

Girard owned a fleet of vessels including the *Montesquieu,* and the *Rousseau* and *Desdemona* which remain to be seen today. They each seem unbelievably small for such long and important voyages. The correspondance of Stephen Girard has been preserved and microfilmed at the American Philosophic Society in Philadelphia and provides one of the best primary sources for economic trade of the period. Girard's many interests were vital to American commerce.

Between 1804 and 1807, of the twelve American ships which took on opium at Smyrna, seven came from Philadelphia, three from Baltimore, and two from Boston. American merchants purchased as much of the Smyrna crop as they could. As a result of the initiation of an American opium trade, Philadelphia merchants became less reliant on the British Levant Company in Smyrna and established agencies of their own in that port. In 1811, David Offley, of the Philadelphia shipping firm of Woodmas and Offley, settled permanently in Smyrna and established the first American commercial house in the Levant. Thirty-four of the seventy-eight American vessels that traded at Smyrna between 1811 and 1820 were consigned to Woodmas and Offley. The remainder were consigned to such native Smyrna merchants as Dutilh and Company, who sent one of their kinsmen, Edward Dutilh, to Philadelphia in 1819 to facilitate stateside aspects of the commerce.[33]

Between 1805 and 1807, Americans annually sold in Canton between one hundred and two hundred chests of Smyrna opium worth between $100,000 and $200,000.

In the years after 1815, American shipments of Smyrna opium to China quadrupled over previous levels. Despite this dramatic upsurge, for the duration of the American Smyrna opium trade, Britain annually shipped to China approximately twenty times as much Indian opium as the Americans were ever able to secure in Turkey.[34]

Despite the small scale of opium shipments, the drug did fulfill merchants' need for a reliable China trade commodity. It was perhaps because of opium's unique qualities that merchants were reluctant to give it up even in the face of official Chinese opposition. In addition to being highly valued by the Chinese, opium had the unusual property of generating an ever increasing demand for itself, at a consistently high price. It was very expensive relative to its bulk, and in this respect almost as valuable as coinage of which there was an extreme scarcity in America. Perhaps most important for many American merchants, opium was a commodity whose shipment could be readily integrated with extant trans Atlantic commerce. Without opium, the tea, silk and porcelain trades could have existed only on a very low level.

American participation in the opium trade continued up through the outbreak of Sino-British hostilities in 1839. During war over this illegal commerce, American merchants kept a pledge to abstain from the opium traffic, and augmented their fortunes through the carriage of British trade. No sooner had hostilities ended than the illicit trade resumed in full force all along the China coast. The end of the foreign opium trade to China came early in the twentieth century, when the Chinese government bowed to the interest of native Chinese opium growers and imposed such high import duties on the drug that the Indian, British, and American traders were forced from the trade entirely.[35] At this time, also ended any large quantity of porcelain importation from China to the United States.

The trade in Chinese porcelain in America throughout the first forty years of the nineteenth century had enjoyed brisk sales of both special order and standard pattern services. Most of the special order sets date from this period and their variety was limited only by the imaginations of the customers. Patriotic themes on porcelain dominated the decorations and reflected the popular tastes. During these decades, the English government imposed a duty of 100% on porcelain imports to

A manifest of the *Missouri*, probably after a trip from Philadelphia to Canton in 1802, mentioning many boxes of chinaware. *(Courtesy: Philadelphia Maritime Museum)*

Opposite: The receipt for a dinner set of "Canton China" purchased in 1825.

THE ENTIRE CARGO

OF THE

SHIP MISSOURI, FROM CANTON,

FOR SALE

On MONDAY next, the 22d instant, at 10 o'clock in the morning, at WILLING'S & FRANCIS'S Stores.

JOHN CONNELLY, Auctioneer.

No 199 Market Street Philad. January 13 1825

Mr Jacob N. Haldeman

Bought of READ & GRAY

Importers of China, Glass, & Queens Ware

1 Dinner Set Canton China		$40 00
Contents as follows		
12 dishes, 8. 10. 12. 14. 16. 18. 20 Inch	12 pcs	
4 doz large flat plates	48.	
2 " large Soup Ditto	24.	
2 " desert Ditto half deep	24.	
2 " relish Ditto Ditto	24.	
1 Soup Tureen Stand & Cover	3.	
2 Sauce Ditto Do Do	6 ..	
2 Sauce Bowls	2.	
1 Hash Dish & hot Water Pan	3 .	
3 round Pudding dishes	3 ..	
1 Sallad Dish	1 .	
2 Square Cover'd Vegatable Dishes	4 .	
1 doz Custard Cups & Covers	24.	
4 Salts	4 .	
	182 pcs	
1 Pair extra Vegatable Dishes with Covers		3 75
1 doz best plain Wines		1 50
1 " Egg Glasses		1 00
Package &c		75
		$47 00
Cash		30 00
		$77 00

764. 68
77 .
£687 . 68

Received Payt.

Read & Gray

protect their growing porcelain industry. Therefore, the special order business in Canton was dominated by the American and European trade. The advertisement for the sale of the cargo of the American ship *Missouri*, probably of 1802, demonstrates the variety of goods which were available. Fans, tortoise shell combs, shirts, handkerchiefs, thread, yardgoods, sugar, indigo and tea were sold along with many boxes of chinaware. The receipt for a dinner set of "Canton China" purchased January 13, 1825, by Mr. Jacob W. Haldemen from the Philadelphia firm of Read and Gray, enumerates one hundred and eighty-two pieces selling for forty dollars. So popular was American interest in China at this period that small museums of Chinese goods sprang up in Boston and Philadelphia. One such museum was started by Robert Waln, Jr. in Philadelphia after his return from China. Waln also published an ambitions book in 1823, the title page of which reads:

> China; comprehending a view of the origin, antiquity, history, religion, morals, government, laws, population, literature, drama, festivals, games, women, beggars, manners customs, etc. of that empire, with remarks on the European embassies to China and the policy of sending a mission from the United States to the court of Pekin to which is added a commercial appendix containing a synopsis of the trade of Portugal, Holland, England, France, Denmark, Ostend, Sweden, Prussia, Trieste, and Spain, in China and India; and a full description of the American trade to Canton, its rise, progress and present state: with mercantile information, useful to the Chinese trader and general merchant.

"China Cottage" of Nathan Dunn, Mount Holly, New Jersey, 1832. *(Courtesy: J. Goldstein)*

CHINA:

COMPREHENDING A VIEW OF THE ORIGIN, ANTIQUITY, HISTORY, RELIGION, MORALS, GOVERNMENT, LAWS, POPULATION, LITERATURE, DRAMA, FESTIVALS, GAMES, WOMEN, BEGGARS, MANNERS, CUSTOMS, &c. OF THAT EMPIRE.

WITH REMARKS

ON THE

EUROPEAN EMBASSIES TO CHINA,

AND THE

POLICY OF SENDING A MISSION

FROM THE UNITED STATES TO THE COURT OF PEKIN.

TO WHICH IS ADDED,

A COMMERCIAL APPENDIX,

CONTAINING

A SYNOPSIS OF THE TRADE OF PORTUGAL, HOLLAND, ENGLAND, FRANCE, DENMARK, OSTEND, SWEDEN, PRUSSIA, TRIESTE, AND SPAIN, IN CHINA AND INDIA;

AND A FULL DESCRIPTION

OF THE

AMERICAN TRADE TO CANTON,

ITS RISE, PROGRESS, AND PRESENT STATE: WITH MERCANTILE INFORMATION, USEFUL TO THE CHINESE TRADER AND GENERAL MERCHANT.

BY ROBERT WALN, Jr.

PHILADELPHIA:

PRINTED AND PUBLISHED FOR THE AUTHOR,
BY J. MAXWELL.

1823.

Title page of Robert Waln, Jr.'s 1823 book. *(Courtesy: J. Goldstein)*

Such a book was taken very seriously by the American public and its ideas about China infiltrated the American society. In 1832, Nathan Dunn of Mount Holly, New Jersey, had architect John Notman design for him a "Chinese Cottage." The schematic elevation was reproduced in A. J. Downing's book *A Treatise on the Theory and Practice of Landscape Gardening*, published in 1841 (New York and London: Willy and Putnam).

After the peace treaty of 1842–44, the highly regulated trade through the Canton cohongs was replaced by open markets in Canton, Amoy, Foochow, Nanking and Shanghai, as well as in the British Crown Colony of Hong Kong. Hong Kong had the finest natural harbor facilities on the China coast. In 1848, regular transpacific steamer service was inaugurated between Hong Kong, the Hawaiian Islands and San Francisco. The completion of the first trans-American railroads shortly thereafter eliminated the need of sailing around the Capes to China. East Coast cities could import China goods more cheaply overland from the West Coast than by a direct sea route from China.

An old China-trade firm wishing to remain in business after the First Treaty Settlement had to rapidly undergo at least two transitions. It had to expand its Chinese operation to at least Hong Kong and Shanghai, if not to all of the open ports. Most American China-trade firms were able to complete this first phase shortly after 1842. Firms were also faced with the necessity of developing new facilities on the American West Coast. By 1846, firms, branches or outlets also had to be established in New York, which had become the port which handled virtually all direct Asiatic maritime shipping to the East Coast.

Small entrepreneurs could not make all of these costly and extensive transitions. The weeding out of the weak from the strong, a process evident in the old China trade as far back as 1821, took on a new impetus as a result of the First Treaty Settlement. Among the few small firms able to make the transition were Wetmore and Company (which ultimately succumbed to bankruptcy in 1856) and the dynamic two-man firm of John D. Sword and Company. They competed in a new China trade dominated by a few shipping giants with fleets of vessels and world-wide buying and marketing apparatuses: Jardine, Sassoon, Olyphant, Heard, Russell and its offspring, the Shanghai Steam Navigation Company.

After 1848, just as New York came to handle virtually all the direct China trade to the American East Coast, San Francisco rose to prominence as the major port for West Coast China commerce. That trade pattern remained essentially unchanged from 1848 until 1950, when the United States embargoed all maritime trade with the newly formed People's Republic of China. That embargo was modified as a result of Chinese-American negotiations in the 1970's. American ships once again began docking at the old treaty ports of the China coast, but originating from such new and diverse locations as Port Seatrain and Pascagoula, as well as established ports of the American East Coast.

Porcelain exportation to the United States had declined by the time of the opium wars. Massive social dislocation with China itself commenced with the outbreak of hostilities in 1839 but endured for the remainder of the nineteenth century. In 1833–34, a mere 1,322 crates of chinaware left Canton for America. Rare references to chinaware occurred in post-1825 business correspondence. The development of a native American porcelain industry in the 1830's appears to have contributed to the decline in chinaware importation. By 1844, native American porcelain factories had taken root and produced products on a far larger scale than had Bonnin and Morris of Philadelphia in the 1770's.[36] The two major early nineteenth century U. S. porcelain factories were those of William Ellis Tucker of Philadelphia and the Bennington works in Vermont. European porcelain had also improved and was competitive with Chinese in terms of price and quality. In the U. S. market these conditions combined to produce a situation in 1850 where special order porcelain had slackened off with the exception of the standard patterns and forms. By the end of this period, tea became the single most important U. S. import from China.[37]

Throughout the period of American-Chinese trade, porcelain shipments continued to make up only a small fraction of overall China trade cargo. The largest single shipment of porcelain seems to have been aboard the *Trident* of New York, with 5,800 piculs of china. The *Empress of China* was about mid-range, with 962 piculs on her 1785 voyage.

Among the Chew family papers preserved at the family's home, Cliveden, in

Philadelphia,[38] are many documents pertinent to the porcelain trade in America. One is a memo written in 1811 as an order for sets of export porcelain. The entire contents of the memo is important to this discussion.

Mrs. B. Chew requests her Friend Mr. B. C. (Benjamin Chew) Wilcocks to procure for her at Canton and to forward to her by the earliest opportunity to Philadelphia directed for B. Chew the following articles conformable to the Patterns accompanying this Memorandum—

60 Tea Cups and Saucers
24 Coffee Cups with one handle and Saucers   } according to Pattern
 2 Bowls holding about a Gallon each   accompanying this -
12 Bowls from a quart to smaller sizes—

60 Shallow Plates
48 Deep or Soup Plates   } according to the
48 Desert Shallow Plates   Pattern of the Plate
48 Desert deep Plates   accompanying this
24 Small plates used as Fruit Plates after dinner   Memo—

2 Dishes for Dinner of 22 Inches in length
2   Dᵒ   –   Dᵒ   –   20 Incs   – Dᵒ
2   Dᵒ   –   Dᵒ   –   18 Incs   – Dᵒ   } corresponding with the
2   Dᵒ   –   Dᵒ   –   16 Incs   – Dᵒ   Pattern of the Plate sent
2   Dᵒ   –   Dᵒ   –   14 Incs   – Dᵒ   except that the Shape
2   Soup   Tureens   and Dishes   of the Dishes meant for
6   round   Dishes   about 9 Incs over   Meat Dishes is to be
2   Dᵒ   –   Dᵒ – about 8 Incs over   after the usual form
                                                 as thus ⬭

One Hundred and Twenty Spanish Dollars are herewith sent - if that amount should not be sufficient B. Chew will pay any extra amount in any way B. C. Wilcocks may direct him—if it should more than sufficient B. C. Wilcocks will be good eno' to add any articles that he may think will be useful in his friend Mrs. C's family.
Philadelphia 25 June 1811.[39]

Mrs B. Chew requests her Friend Mr B. C. Wilcocks to procure for her at Canton and to forward to her by the earliest opportunity to Philadelphia directed for B. Chew the following Articles conformable to the Patterns accompanying this Memorandum —

60   Tea Cups and Saucers   } according to Pattern
24   Coffee Cups with one handle & Saucers   } accompanying this —
2   Bowls holding about a Gallon, each
12   Bowls from a quart to smaller sizes —

60   Shallow Plates   } according to the
48   Deep or Soup Plates   } Pattern of the Plate
48   Desert Shallow Plates   } accompanying this
48   Desert deep Plates   } Memo —
24   Small plates used as Fruit Plates after dinner

2   Dishes for Dinner of 22 Inches in length   } corresponding with the
2   Do - Do - 20 Incˢ - Do   } Pattern of the Plate sent
2   Do - Do - 18 Incˢ - Do   } except that the Shape
2   Do - Do - 16 Incˢ - Do   } of the Dishes meant for
2   Do - Do - 14 Incˢ - Do   } Meat Dishes is to be
2   Soup Tureens & Dishes   } after the usual form
6   round Dishes about 9 Incˢ over   } as this
2   Do - Do - about 8 Incˢ over

One Hundred and Twenty Spanish Dollars are herewith sent — if that amount should not be sufficient B. Chew will pay any extra amount in any way B. C. Wilcocks may direct him — if it should more than sufficient B. C. Wilcocks will be good eno' to add any articles that he may think will be useful in his Friend Mrs C's Family.

Philadelphia 25 June 1811 —

26

The Chew family home "Cliveden" may be typical of households where several sets of Chinese porcelain services were used during the nineteenth century. *(Courtesy: Cliveden, The National Trust for Historic Preservation)*

The dining room at Cliveden is set for Dessert with a monogrammed Chinese porcelain service. *(Courtesy: Cliveden, The National Trust for Historic Preservation)*

Six different Chinese porcelain table services have been retained at Cliveden near Philadelphia by generations of the Chew family; Rose Medallion, Mandarin, Canton, Fitzhugh, classical figures and a monogrammed set. *(Courtesy: Cliveden, The National Trust for Historic Preservation)*

Mrs. Chew ran a large household in the Germantown section of Philadelphia at "Cliveden" - now preserved as a museum by the National Trust for Historic Preservation. Here consecutive generations of the Chew and Collateral families kept house with numerous sets of Chinese export porcelain. Two of early recorded sets appear on a letter dated Canton, 14th March, 1804, as three boxes containing for B. Chew Esquire:

1 Dinner set of	105 pieces		
1 Dessert D°	48 D°		
6 Pots au Chamber	6		
6 Wash H(and)Basons and Jugs	12		
6 Pitchers	6		
4 Mugs	4		
4 New fashioned affairs	4		
	185 pieces	Cost	$100.00

And for B. Chew Junior Esquire:

3 Boxes chinaware	$ 75.00

The variety of dinner services represented in this house include a wide range of the special order and mass produced patterns. To this day, pieces from six services are remaining at Cliveden. One monogram decorated service remains with a gold script "C" in an eight pointed star. An unusual dessert service is also represented with classically inspired vases around the edge, and a seated female with dog as the main decoration. Besides these, which were probably ordered by the family specifically, there are also the standard export wares of Fitzhugh, Canton, Mandarin, and Rose Medallion decorations. Variations of Chinese porcelain are still being found by excavations of the yard around Cliveden.

The investigation of these various services of porcelain made for American families takes one into the artistic, commercial and political history of the country. People are so curiously connected to one another through marriages, business associations, location and personal interests that it isn't long before names appear in different contexts again and again. The porcelain tells many stories of the country and times in which it was created.

Armorial decorations

Fragments of this plate were excavated on the site of the Governor's Palace in Williamsburg, Virginia, before restoration was begun. The arms are those of Lord Dunmore, the last colonial governor of Virginia from 1771 to 1775. John Murray, Earl of Dunmore (1732–1809) was reared in the ancestral home in Scotland. In 1770, he was appointed governor of the royal colony of New York and paid from revenues collected from the tax on tea. In 1771, he was promoted by appointment as governor of Virginia at the palace in Williamsburg. Conflicts here between loyal and revolutionary factions grew until January 1, 1776 when he fled to England. From 1787 to 1796 he was governor of the Bahamas. *(Courtesy: Colonial Williamsburg).*

The arms of Handcock appear on this mug of the 1790 period with the motto "Obsta principiis". The family originated in Combe Martin, Devon, England, and the coat of arms was confirmed to the family of Nathaniel Hancock, who was at Cambridge, Massachusetts in 1652. It is most probable that he was related to the East India Company merchant Nathaniel Hancock, who was at Canton in 1747. America's patriot John Hancock (1737–1793) was related to this family and used this coat of arms. *(Courtesy: The Henry Francis du Pont Winterthur Museum).*

In 1681, William Penn was granted land on the west side of the Delaware River in North America, by Charles II, in recognition of Penn's father's services and debts owed by the Crown at his death. This land was called Pennsylvania. William Penn's second son, Thomas Penn of Stoke Park, Buckingham shire, in 1751 married Lady Juliana Fermor, the 4th daughter of the Earl of Pomfret. This Chinese porcelain service, with the arms of the Penn family, was probably made for this son. Thomas Penn succeeded his mother, Hannah, and brother, John, as chief proprietor of Pennsylvania until 1775. *(Courtesy: Phil Cooke Collection)*

This soup dish was made for Samuel Vaughan soon after his marriage to Sarah Hallowell of Boston in 1747. The central decoration is the coat of arms of Vaughan impaling Hallowell inscribed, 'Samuel Vaughan' and motto "In Prudentia et Simpliceiate". It is copied from an engraved book plate with different motto that was designed for Samuel Vaughan by Thomas Chippendale. The rim is painted *en grisaille* and gold with four vignettes of Chinese bird and landscape motifs.[40] *(Courtesy: The National Museum of History and Technology, Smithsonian Institution).*

This plate is from a service of more than two hundred and sixty pieces[41] made about 1795 for Jeremiah Townley Chase (d. 1828). His paternal grandmother was Lady Margaret Townley who married Richard Chase of Annapolis, Maryland in 1714. The Townley coat of arms was adapted for the Chase family.[42] *(Courtesy: Maryland Historical Society)*

This 16″ diameter platter belonged to Major Russell Sturgis of Smith Point, Manchester, Massachusetts. The initials 'A. B. W.'(?) are joined with a crest of three axes and three red chevrons in a shield. The platter was probably part of a service bought by William Sturgis in Canton to commemorate a wedding in the family. William Sturgis (1782–1863) was an active merchant of the Massachusetts Sturgis shipping family. At the age of nineteen he became master of the *Caroline* and in 1809 fought pirates on the *Atahualpa* off the Chinese coast. In 1810 he formed a partnership with John Bryant of Boston. During the fifty-three years of their association he built a fortune. A large percent of the U.S. to China trade between 1810 and 1840 was under their direction. William Sturgis also served in the Massachusetts legislature in 1814 and 1846, and was president of the Marine Society and Massachusetts Historical Society. *(Courtesy: Russell Scheider Antiques, Merrimack, New Hampshire)*

The Morton bowl has become a well-known example of American market porcelain. With a capacity for eight gallons of punch, this twenty-one and three-eighth inch diameter bowl is ten inches high, and therefore one of the largest remaining punch bowls with American connections. The inscriptions on the bowl explain most of what is known about it. The exterior is inscribed around the rim, "Presented by General Jacob Morton to the corporation of the city of New York, July 4, 1812." At the foot it reads, "This bowl was made by syngchong in Canton, Fungmanhi Pinxt." The interior rim is inscribed twice, "Drink deep. You will preserve the city and encourage canals." The exterior of the punch bowl is further decorated with four scenes, two small views of the New York harbor, the seal of the United States and the seal of New York City.

The interior view of New York is a direct copy of the engraving shown here which was made by Samuel Seymour after William Birch's painting and published January 1, 1803. The Chinese painters were extremely competent copyists as a comparison of details will verify here.

This connection between Chinese porcelain decoration, Samuel Seymour engravings and William Birch paintings was made again with the Mount Vernon scene in the section on Western landscapes in this book. Seymour and Birch lived and worked near one another, northwest of Philadelphia, producing American landscape scenes of popular interest. *(Courtesy: The Metropolitan Museum of Art, lent by the city of New York, 1912)*

The City of
New York IN THE STATE OF NEW YORK North America

This print "New York from Brooklyn, 1803", was engraved by Samuel Seymour after a painting by William Birch. It is the source of the Chinese painting inside the General Jacob Morton bowl. *(Courtesy: I. N. Phelps Stokes Collection, Prints Division, the New York Public Library; Astor, Lenox and Tilden Foundations).*

Interior, Morton bowl.

The New York State coat of arms can be found with several variations on Chinese dinnerware from the period between 1785 and 1805. The prototype consisted of the figure of Liberty in a blue dress and Justice in a white dress with their symbols flanking a medallion with vine border, a rising sun and seven hills in the medallion resting over two American shields and a banner inscribed "Excelsior." Variations differ primarily in the decoration of the medallion, being most commonly a floral spray or a monogram in a shield. The official New York coat of arms was devised in 1777 and adopted in 1778 with modifications in 1778, 1798, 1809 and 1882.[43] *(Courtesy: Matthew and Elisabeth Sharpe)*

Note the shields of the United States flanking, and below the New York State shield. *(Courtesy: Matthew and Elisabeth Sharpe)*

The coat of arms of Pennsylvania was adopted in this form on March 2, 1809 with the motto "Virtue, Liberty, Independence". The initials "P.M." appear on the bottom of the cup, presumably being those of the unknown original owner. This is one of the rarest services, which might seem surprising since so much China—America trade had Pennsylvania connections.[44] *(Courtesy: The New York Historical Society).*

The early emblem of New Hampshire was painted on this tea service for John A. Colby of Concord, New Hampshire approximately between 1790 and 1810. On February 12, 1785 the New Hampshire legislature adopted the emblem of a rising sun and unmasted ship on the stocks of a shipyard. The emblem was revised in 1931 with a broadside view of the frigate *Raleigh*, on the stocks, with three lower masts, pennants and flags. This service has always been accompanied by a bill for fifty-three pieces of porcelain from the merchant Yam Shinqua of Canton.[45] *(Courtesy: The Henry Francis du Pont Winterthur Museum).*

This bowl is ornamented with the American eagle and shield, possibly depicting the early version of the state seal of Illinois.[46] Illinois joined the Union in 1818 and adopted a revised seal in 1867. The decoration on this bowl is of the Federal period in character but it was probably made in the second quarter of the nineteenth century. A similar decoration appears on the Surrender of Burgoyne and Declaration of Independence pieces in the section on political decoration (see pages 144–149). *(Courtesy: The Bayou Bend Collection of the Museum of Fine Arts, Houston)*

The lady and anchor above the oval cartouche are the traditional emblems of HOPE, as a naval heroine. They are sometimes associated with the State seal of Rhode Island[47] and may therefore further the identification of this "Smith" to Henry Smith of Providence, Rhode Island, who was an officer of the ship *George Washington* on a voyage in 1794. The ship was owned by John Brown and John Francis of Providence. A bowl in the Winterthur collection is decorated with an anchor in a shield below a ribbon inscribed "In God We Hope" and an interior inscription "Henry Smith, Canton, 1794", apparently for whom it was made. *(Courtesy: (bowl) Anonymous; (plate) The Henry Francis duPont Winterthur Museum)*

This pair of garniture vases bears the name of "Allen B. Strong" at the bottom of the cartouche. He is presumed to have lived in New Jersey about 1800. There is a pensive figure seated above his name in the cartouche. On the side of the vases are two cartouches—the upper with a western landscape view, the lower an Oriental bird sitting in a tree. The predominant colors are brown, gold, blue, green, black and pink on the clothes of the seated figure. *(Courtesy: Herbert Schiffer Antiques)*.

The porcelain dinner service which was made for John Stark (1728–1822) of Londonderry, New Hampshire is decorated with two shields, each surmounted by a bird over bar sinister. One shield encloses a sheaf of wheat, the bearing of the Stark family from Ulster County, Ireland. The other shield encloses a sun rising over mountains signifying John Stark's leadership in 1777 at a battle near Bennington, Vermont where British troops were defeated. The dinner service dates from the first decade of the nineteenth century so was made to commemorate John Stark's brilliant military career. His military career during the French and Indian War and American Revolution included service with Rogers' Rangers, as colonel of a New Hampshire regiment at Bunker Hill, in the defense of New York, Trenton, Princeton, and later near Bennington. He retired to his home in New Hampshire while declining offers to hold public office. *(Courtesy: The Bennington Museum).*

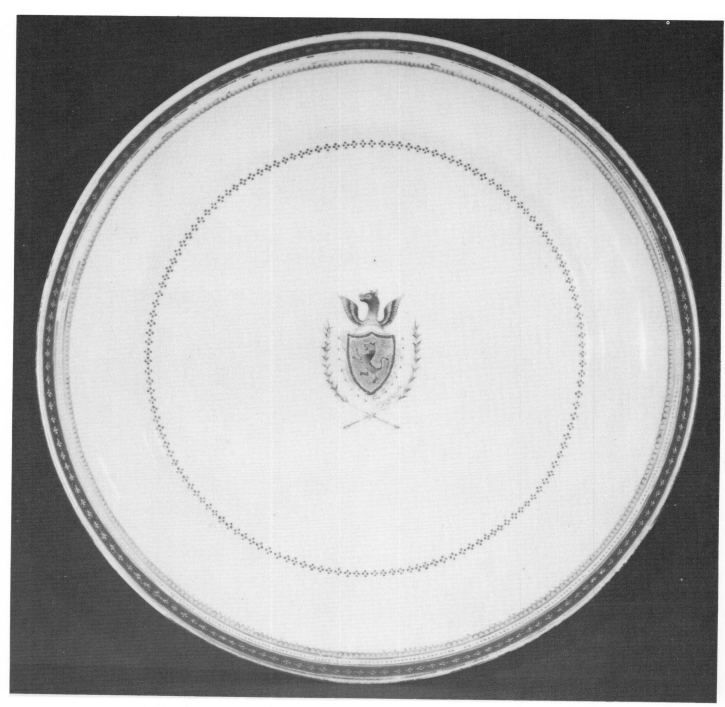

This plate is part of a service made circa 1784 for John Morgan of Hartford, Connecticut and brought back on the *Empress of China* on which his nephew of the same name served as a carpenter, and died on the return voyage. It is inscribed below the shield "Morgan." *(Courtesy: Museum of the American China Trade)*

An almost identical plate has "Elias Morgan" inscribed below the shield and a history in the same Morgan family of Connecticut. This service probably was made for the elder John's brother Elias a few years later.[48] *(Courtesy: The Henry Francis duPont Winterthur Museum)*

The arms of the Sargent family of Boston and New York appear on this plate with the motto *Nec quaerere Honorem, Nec Spernere* (Neither to seek nor to despise honors). Bookplates of Ignatius Sargent and Winthrop Sargent both have this same design.[49]

Winthrop Sargent (1753–1820) was from Gloucester, Massachusetts, served in the Continental Army, surveyed Ohio and became an effective administrator of the territory west of Ohio. In 1798 he became the first governor of the Mississippi territory.[50] Plate, 6 1/4 inches diameter, circa 1785–90. *(Courtesy: Museum of the American China Trade)*

This tureen and platter are part of a Chinese porcelain dinner service given to Elias Boudinot IV (1740–1821) by the Continental Congress in recognition of his service as President of the Congress.[51] Because Boudinot lived in Princeton, New Jersey and was a Trustee of Princeton University, he brought the Congress to Nassau Hall, at the University, when unpaid troops were harassing the Congress in Philadelphia. Nassau Hall served as the capitol for the new nation for several months. Elias Boudinot IV was elected to the House of Representatives in the first, second and third Congresses. In 1795 he became director of the United States Mint. He was the first counsellor named by the United States Supreme Court. A pair of urns which have descended with this service are shown on page 76. *(Courtesy: The Art Museum, Princeton University)*

Elias Haskett Derby (1739–1799) of Salem, Massachusetts, owned merchant ships in the late 18th century and carried on an active and highly successful trade in the West Indies for spices, including pepper and coffee. He established routes to St. Petersburg, Russia; Manila; Batavia; Rangoon; Calcutta and Bombay, India; and became one of the wealthiest merchants in New England. In 1785–6 he entered the China trade with *The Grand Turk,* sailing from Salem to the Cape of Good Hope, Isle of France in the Indian Ocean, and on to Canton. This was the first New England ship to reach the Orient. Derby ordered, apparently on this trip, a set of porcelain dinnerware and tea service numbering 272 pieces, decorated with his initials, the figure of Hope with an anchor, and the motto "*Spero*" (Hope). A tureen from this service illustrates a preference at the end of the 18th century for open, floral patterns. Derby's career is most interesting and spans the development of the China trade through its rise in international commerce.

Two other services which apparently also returned on this voyage of *The Grand Turk* are shown in the monogram section, page 59. *(Courtesy: The Henry Francis duPont Winterthur Museum)*

The arms of Alexander quartering MacDonald appear on this plate intended for Major-General William Alexander (1726–1783). In America he was known as Lord Sterling, but his claim to the Earldom of Sterling was not recognized in England. The dinner service of which this was a part was never delivered to Alexander because of his death. His military career was an impressive list of commands in New Jersey and New York as well as Valley Forge, Brandywine, Germantown and Philadelphia. He had many successful business interests on which his fortune was based. *(Courtesy: Museum of the American China Trade)*

The decoration on this cider jug combines the full Fitzhugh pattern with the coat of arms of the Clements family of Philadelphia. The same family owned the pair of Monteith bowls with their coat of arms and grapevine border. *(Courtesy: Nantucket Historical Association).*

This monteith, one of two known from the same set, was made for the Philadelphia Clements family. It bears their coat of arms and is believed to have been made circa 1790–1800 when the grapevine border was copied from English pattern books. *(Courtesy: Nantucket Historical Association).*

The sepia Fitzhugh open serving dish includes the arms of the Goldsborough family of Maryland and motto "Non Sibi". Prominent members of this family include Robert Goldsborough (1733–1788), lawyer and member of the Continental Congress; Charles Goldsborough (1765–1834), last Federalist governor of Maryland from 1818 to 1819; and Louis Malesherbes Goldsborough (1805–1877), a naval officer. *(Courtesy: Museum of the American China Trade).*

Charles Izard Manigault (1795–1874) of Charleston, South Carolina traveled to Canton and the Far East between 1817 and 1823. During this time, he sent back home a service of Chinese porcelain decorated in sepia Fitzhugh with his family coat of arms. The armorial crest was copied from a design by an engraver, S. Clayton, in New South Wales. Clayton added to the arms a crescent indicating Charles as the second son.[52] To his older brother, Gabriel Henry (1789–1834), Charles sent another porcelain service which is shown in the monogram section of this book (see page 61). *(Courtesy: Herbert Schiffer Antiques)*

The unusual reticulated fruit basket is painted in detail with a trellis design of the late 18th century and a variation of the Lee family coat of arms. This basket has survived with a history in the Lee family of Virginia, and well could have been a design conceived by one of their members circa 1790. Included among the illustrious Lees is the brilliant soldier Henry (Light Horse Harry), (1756–1818) who owned a service of Order of the Cincinnati porcelain (see page 134). Therefore, he may be responsible for this service as well. He was the father of the Confederate general Robert E. Lee who may well have owned Chinese porcelain, but probably of a later style. *(Courtesy: Theodore H. Kapnek, Sr.)*

This covered vegetable dish has a finial sometimes found on Fitzhugh. The sprig designs are those often found on English porcelain of the end of the 18th century and beginning of the 19th century such as Minton. The animal over the initial "W" identifies this as part of a set made for the Winthrops of Boston. *(Courtesy: Museum of Fine Arts, Boston).*

The two-handled urn (circa 1785–90) bears the coat of arms of James Duane and the initials of his wife Mary Alexander Livingston Duane. James Duane was the first mayor of New York City after the Revolution from 1784 to 1789. He defended Lieutenant Governor Colden when the Crown, in the person of Lord Dunmore, sued Colden in Chancery for half a year's fees while Colden had been acting in Lord Dunmore's stead. Lord Dunmore, as Chancellor, presided over the trial when he himself was plaintiff. Mary Livingston Duane was the daughter of Robert Livingston, the "third lord" of Livingston Manor, and married Duane in 1759. *(Courtesy: Bernard and S. Dean Levy, Inc.)*

Monogrammed decorations

In America, discontinued use of Armorial crests caused use of initials to specify the ownership of property. Families with no crest could not be readily distinguished from armigerous families here. Therefore, single and multiple initials are commonly found on special order porcelain made for American families.

The two similar saucers with central painted decoration of Minerva and cupid were apparently made at the same time in Canton as parts of two tea services. The decoration is a copy of an engraving. The left example is initialed "JD" for J. Derby, a member of the Derby family of Salem, Massachusetts. The right example is initialed "DFA" for Deborah Fairfax Anderson, also of Salem. Both sets were brought from Canton on the *Grand Turk's* first trip to China in 1786. Elias Hasket Derby owned the *Grand Turk* and another porcelain service with his own crest, shown on page 52, which also apparently came to Salem on this same trip. *(Courtesy: Peabody Museum of Salem)*

This plate is decorated with gilt design "New York, 1793, EAL". It most probably was made for a member of the Livingston family of New York. It is one of the few dated pieces remaining. 7 7/8″ diameter. *(Courtesy: The Henry Francis du Pont Winterthur Museum).*

The monogram "CFCS" below a bird over bar sinister crest has not been identified but the dinner service from which this comes has a history in a family from Charleston, South Carolina. *(Courtesy: The Charleston Museum)*

The monogram "GHM" are those of Gabriel Henry Manigault (1789–1834), of Charleston, South Carolina, whose brother Charles Izard Manigault lived in the Far East between 1817 and 1823. During this period he sent Gabriel the dinner service from which these pieces come. The sepia Fitzhugh decoration is meticulously painted, and the monogram replaces the family's armorial crest. The belt which surrounds the monogram bears the motto *Praspicere Quam Ulcisci* (It is better to anticipate than to avenge).[5][3] The American Indian figure above the crest also appears on a service Charles had made for himself which is shown in the armorial section of this book (see page 56). *(Courtesy: Herbert Schiffer Antiques)*

61

The center of the star on this bowl is embellished with gold initials "J.A." for John Amory of Boston. He was a descendant of Thomas Amory (1682–1728), an immigrant from Ireland who became a merchant in the West Indies and Charleston, South Carolina, and finally resided in Boston. Here he built a wharf and still house, distilled rum and turpentine, developed a successful trade inland and abroad, and conducted a shipbuilding firm. He married Rebecca Holmes in 1721. *(Courtesy: Museum of Fine Arts, Boston).*

Thomas Mason of Philadelphia and Charleston was a ship's captain of some notoriety. During the American Revolution, he risked a trip to France with introductions and connections through Thomas Jefferson and Benjamin Franklin and brought back gun powder for the American army. In 1766 he married Priscilla Sisom of Philadelphia. This punch bowl monogrammed "TM" has been kept in the Mason family with associated furniture to recent times. The sunburst decoration and edge bands are motifs of the late eighteenth century, circa 1790. *(Courtesy: a private collection)*

This bowl was made for Stephen Girard of Philadelphia and bears his initials. Girard's life is so interesting and pertinent to this study, yet only a few comments can be made here. The interested readers are directed to the bibliography for additional material. Stephen Girard (1750–1831) was a Ferich immigrant to America who went to sea at fourteen and developed a career as merchant, financier and philanthropist. He managed a highly successful trade with the West Indies from Philadelphia and Mount Holly, New Jersey. He owned eighteen vessels during his career but only six at one time, maximum. His interest in the China trade grew with characteristic caution. His first launch to the East was in 1796 when the brig *Sally* left Philadelphia for the Isle of France (Mauritius). In 1802, Girard's *Rousseau* left for Canton with a cargo of ginseng and returned in 1804 with a cargo that sold for a phenomenal profit.[54] Fifteen voyages to Canton followed between 1804 and 1824. Other plates owned by Girard are shown on page 187. *(Courtesy: The Stephen Girard Collection)*

The wide sepia, black and gold border on this syllabub cup lid is derived from the English Leeds pottery factory design books which enjoyed wide distribution world wide. Many American market sets of the first quarter of the nineteenth century have this on a variation border, often in combination with a Fitzhugh decoration. The service from which this cup comes is decorated in sepia tones and was made for David and Ann Pingree of New England about 1820. *(Courtesy: The Peabody Museum of Salem)*

The initials "MLRF" are those of Mary Livinia and Rodney Fisher of Delaware. These are part of a service made circa 1810–20. Rodney Fisher (1798–1863) was distinguished as a U.S. Navy midshipman and later merchant for Edward Thompson of Philadelphia, in Canton for the English firm McVicar & Co., and in India. He returned to Philadelphia in 1845. *(Courtesy: The Henry Francis du Pont Winterthur Museum).*

This teapot is decorated with an all-over geometric pattern and bird-crested oval reserves more similar to early nineteenth century porcelain sets than the majority of sets made for America. The round medallion is monogrammed "JG" for James Gibson of Baltimore, Maryland to whom the dinnerware was given by his wife Mary Jackson. *(Courtesy: Museum of Early Southern Decorative Arts).*

This is one of more than a hundred surviving pieces of a porcelain dinner set given by Robert Morris to John Nixon circa 1800. Nixon (1733–1808) was a Philadelphia shipping merchant of the firm Nixon and Walker. His political interests led him into national service. In 1775 he became a member of the provincial Committee of Safety where he acted as president when the President Benjamin Franklin and Vice President Robert Morris were absent. *(Courtesy: Private Collection).*

The initials of Thomas McKean (1734–1817) embellish this bowl on the interior bottom and both sides. The bowl and a few related pieces were made for him in the last ten years of his life.

Thomas McKean was born on a farm in Chester County, Pennsylvania and attended the Rev. Francis Allenson's Academy at New London, Pennsylvania. He then went to New Castle, Delaware to study law, and when he was twenty he was admitted to the bar. He held many offices, including Prothonotary, Assistant Attorney General, member of the state legislature and Judge. McKean was a member of the Continental Congress when he signed the Declaration of Independence. At different times, he was President of Delaware, Governor of Pennsylvania, President of Congress, and Chief Justice of the Pennsylvania Supreme Court for twenty-two years. He also instituted the spoils system into Pennsylvania politics. *(Courtesy: Herbert Schiffer Antiques, Inc.)*

The grape vine border on Chinese porcelain can be found in a variety of color combinations and design combinations. A similar border decoration can be found on a service initialed "P" and made for David M. Perine of Baltimore. This service has been divided into thirds, one part remaining in the family, one part given to the Maryland Historical Society, and one part given to the Henry Francis duPont Winterthur Museum.

Here the grape vine is varied as three borders for initials "JAA" which stand for the original owners John and Abigail Adams. John Adams (1735—1826) and his wife (1744—1818) resided in Quincy, Massachusetts and capital cities during periods of diplomatic missions. Politics was a way of life for this family, leading Adams into service to the country which culminated with his becoming the second President of the United States from 1796—1800. Abigail has achieved a high place among literary critics for her own writing and correspondance through the stormy and productive early years of the nation.

Another of the Adams' porcelain services is shown in color on page 107. *(Courtesy: John Quentin Feller)*

The monogram on this helmet shaped cream pitcher is "T. N." for Thomas Nelson (1738–1789), of Virginia. Nelson was by profession a merchant and statesman, becoming vocal and involved with America's fight for independence. He signed the Declaration of Independence for Virginia. Later he became Virginia's governor and spent his personal fortune for the American cause. *(Courtesy: Mr. and Mrs. Richard M. Stiner).*

The cider jug is part of a large dinner set monogrammed "AST" which originally belonged to Amos Townsend (1773–1855) and his wife Sarah (nee Howe, 1773–1826) who lived in New Haven.[55] The set was given to the Townsends by a cousin Ebenezer Townsend, circa 1799, who was the supercargo on the *Neptune* from New Haven. A bowl showing the ship *Neptune* appears in the section on marine decoration, p. 156. *(Courtesy: The New Haven Colony Historical Society, gift of Anna P. Bradley)*

This tea pot was part of a set presented by the City of Boston to one of the first druggists of the Boston Dispensary, Dr. Oliver Smith. The word "memento" is shown below the initials "OS". This dates from the end of the 18th century. *(Courtesy: Museum of Fine Arts, Boston. Gift of Eveleth C. Cowles in memory of Ann W. Cooper)*

This mug of the period circa 1790 to 1800 bears the initials "HCS" for a member of the Shipley family of Wilmington, Delaware. The decoration is very similar to the previous tea pot for Oliver Smith. *(Courtesy: The National Trust for Historic Preservation)*

The Cypher in the shield reads "MH" for Mary Hemphill Jones, daughter of William Hemphill and wife of Morgan Jones of Delaware. The set was made about 1800–1810. The central painted decoration of a girl and a dog was copied from a contemporary engraving as yet unlocated. *(Courtesy: Daughters of the American Revolution Museum).*

Thomas Jefferson owned a dinner service initialed "J" within a shield with garland manteling shown on page 93.

Very similar to Thomas Jefferson's porcelain decoration is this crest on a service which was made for Governor Gore of Massachusetts. Christopher Gore (1758–1827) graduated from Harvard in 1776, and rose in politics to become governor from 1809 to 1810, and a Massachusetts Senator between 1814 and 1816. His father, John Gore, was a painter and merchant of Boston who married Frances Pinckney Gore in 1743. *(Courtesy: John Quentin Feller)*

The monogram "CVD" stands for the original owner of this tea service, Catherine Vanderpool Van Dyke of Newark, New Jersey. Miss Vanderpool (1741–1823) married Newark merchant James Van Dyke (1740–1828) in 1765. In his will of 1823, proved 1828, the residue of his estate was left to Catherine Van Dyke Parker including "one blue sett tea china, one sett pencil'd do $4.00."

The border decoration is a variation of the Fitzhugh pattern. *(Courtesy: The Newark Museum Collection)*

The sepia and gold patterned rim band surrounds the central shield with light, scrolled leaf and garland supports. The monogram "JAD" is that of John and Ann Donnell of Baltimore. This service dates from about 1810. *(Courtesy: John Quentin Feller)*

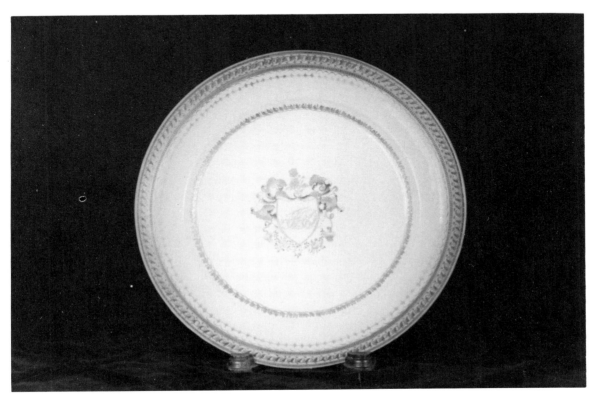

73

This tea caddy is part of a miniature tea service of the 1810—1820 period monogrammed "EF". The original owner is not known but was presumably the fortunate child of a merchant family. There are so few remaining pieces of miniature porcelain, that each example such as this is highly prized today. The mantling here is blue with blue serpentine dotted bands above and below. The intertwined initials are painted in gold. *(Courtesy: T. H. Kapnek, Sr.)*

Right - In the center of the shield are the initials "RES" for Russell and Elisabeth Parkins Sturgis of Manchester, Massachusetts who were married in 1773. The plate is dated because of its overall decoration to the last quarter of the eighteenth century. Another set of this family is shown on page 36. *(Courtesy: Museum of Fine Arts, Boston. Gift of Mrs. H. P. Sturgis)*

The lighthouse-shaped coffee pot is part of twenty pieces remaining from a set of dinnerware brought to Trenton, New Jersey from Canton by Captain Edward Yard (1761–1839). The monogram "EY" is displayed in drapery manteling so popular in the period, circa 1790–1800. *(Courtesy: Old Barracks Association, Trenton, New Jersey)*

This fine pair of pistol handled urns bear the cypher "CB" and have descended in the family of Elias Boudinot IV, whose armorial set of porcelain is shown on p. 51. The initials have not yet been identified with one member of this family, yet in style they represent the popular mantling of the period, circa 1800. Lawyer Elias Boudinot (1740–1821) of Philadelphia, married Hannah Stockton in 1762. Their only child, Susan Vergereau (1764–1854), married William Bradford, attorney-general from 1794–1795. This pair of urns, therefore, may have been made for a Bradford. *(Courtesy: The Art Museum, Princeton University)*

These unusual covered jars have gold and green decoration typical of the early nineteenth century style. The shield bears the monogram "TSS" for a member of the Sears family of Boston. The drapery surrounding the shield is typical of the period when Americans adopted such designs in lieu of armorial crests.

Isaac Sears (1730–1786) was an American Revolutionary leader who commanded his own merchant ships and became a hero when he led a parade of sailors at New York's harbor. Between 1777 and 1783 he lived in Boston running his business ventures. On February 4, 1786 he sailed with Samuel Shaw and Thomas Randall for China to promote trade, but died at Canton of fever in October and was buried on French Island in the Canton harbor. *(Courtesy: Matthew and Elisabeth Sharpe)*

The initials "V.H." stand for a member of the Hunt family of New Haven for whom this dinner service was made, circa 1790–1800. *(Courtesy: The New Haven Colony Historical Society, gift of Mrs. Sarah G. Hunt Jones)*

The border decoration on this small tray is a distinctive combination of dotted bands and sweeping, feather edge which is found on several sets of dishes dating from the 1790 to 1800 period. The border seems to be limited to this time period on the examples noted in this study, and may therefore aid in dating similar sets which are found.

The manteling and shield at the center of this service is monogrammed "SH", and is known to have been made for Samuel Huntington (1731–1796). Huntington was a politically active lawyer from Connecticut who became closely involved in the cause for Revolution in his state. He was one of the signers of the Declaration of Independence, president of the Continental Congress from 1779 to 1781, and governor of Connecticut from 1786 to 1797. *(Courtesy: John Quentin Feller)*

These pieces are part of a dinner service made for the Philadelphian William Phillips about 1795–1805. *(Courtesy of a descendant. Nantucket Historical Association)*

This set of dinnerware was made for Peter and Elizabeth Crary of New York, having their initials "PEC" inscribed on the dark blue central shield. They were made circa 1790–1800. Peter Crary (1781–1842) and Elizabeth Denison Crary (1781–1848) are shown in their portraits. *(Courtesy: Gouverneur Morris Helfenstein)*

Peter Crary

Elizabeth Crary

The monogram arrangement on this plate is unusual for porcelain decoration. The service was made for Robert Hooper and his wife. Hooper (1709—1791) was a merchant of Marblehead, Massachusetts, so popular with his crews that he was known as "King."

The arrangement of the family initial centered above the husband's, and wife's first initial is an old fashioned style found more frequently on silver and inlaid furniture of the eighteenth century. The additional use of a pair of doves above the shield, and symmetrical drapery helps to date the plate in the first few years of the nineteenth century. *(Courtesy: John Quentin Feller)*

The initials "S.B." are those of a member of the Bradley family of New Haven for whom this tea service was made, circa 1790–1800. The use of kissing doves was made popular at this period in America to signify a happy marriage. *(Courtesy: The New Haven Colony Historical Society, gift of F. Thornton Hunt)*

The Fitzhugh pattern was, by the early nineteenth century, a mass-produced decoration made most frequently with blue decoration but also orange, green, sepia, raspberry, yellow, black and gold. This plate is one of the very few surviving blue Fitzhugh pieces with initials of the original owner. The monogram "JWP" stands for Joseph Page White, an owner of ships in Salem, Massachusetts, in the early nineteenth century. Other Fitzhugh services without initials but with documented American family histories, can be found in the floral section, pages 108, 207–208. *(Courtesy: Peabody Museum of Salem)*

The monogram "USG" on this Rose Medallion shrimp dish stands for American President Ulysses Simpson Grant. The three hundred and fifteen piece service from which the plate comes was ordered in 1868 by Mrs. Grant from a merchant in China, Daniel Ammen, as letters which remain document. The service came to New York in April of 1869 and was presumably used by the Grants during their administration at the White House.[56] *(Courtesy: The Henry Francis duPont Winterthur Museum).*

This is a fine example of the early period Rose Medallion decoration with melon-shaped panels in simple outline. The intertwined initials "SW" stand for Stephen G. Wheatland.

There remain parts of an additional service monogrammed "SGW" with Rose Medallion decoration. *(Courtesy: John Quentin Feller)*

This sepia Fitzhugh decorated plate bears the monogram "CMJ" for Catesby and Mary Jones. Thomas Ap Catesby Jones (1790–1858) and Mary Walker Carter were married in 1823, both from prominent families of Virginia. Jones had a distinguished and controversial career in the U.S. Navy. His training under Isaac Hull and Stephen Decatur at Norfolk prepared him for later service suppressing the slave trade, smuggling and piracy and enforcing neutrality laws. In an attack on pirates at Barataria in 1814, he dramatically saved a ship from explosion. Later that year he captured British gunboats and kept American casualties to a low number in a fierce encounter in which he was severely wounded. He commanded the Pacific Squadron three times in 1825, 1842 and 1844 during the Mexican War. *(Courtesy: Museum of Early Southern Decorative Arts, Winston-Salem, North Carolina)*

These handsome covered serving dishes, part of a sweet meat set, are decorated on the tops and inside with a standard Fitzhugh pattern except for the addition of an "H" in a clear field in the center of the medallion.

The "H" stands for Robert Henley (1783–1828) of Virginia whose career as a naval officer was distinguished. He was a nephew of George Washington through the Custis family. At the battle of Lake Champlain in 1814, he won fame for an important part of the American victory. *(Courtesy: Colonial Williamsburg, Williamsburg, Virginia)*

This orange Fitzhugh sauce tureen is particularly interesting because besides "R. Smith" it is inscribed "Mississippi". The state of Mississippi joined the Union in 1817. Since research has not been able to further identify R. Smith, it can only be supposed that the tureen was made at about the 1815-20 period like so much of the other Fitzhugh decorated porcelain. In 1861, Mississippi seceded from the Union for the duration of the Confederacy and rejoined in 1870 according to the congressional plan of reconstruction. *(Courtesy: James Galley)*

This orange Fitzhugh covered vegetable dish, circa 1800, is monogrammed in gold "EAT" for Edward (1771–1853) and Ann Renshaw Thomson (1773–1842) of Philadelphia who were married in 1796. *(Courtesy: Philadelphia Museum of Art. Bequest of Mrs. Harry Markoe)*

The reticulated fruit basket and plate are part of a sixty-five piece green Fitzhugh dinner service monogrammed "JCR" and "R" respectively. The family story which has survived with them explains that a member of the Leedom family of Philadelphia, probably Jonathan Leedom (1775–1848), sent to China a similar plate with the initial "R" to be copied but with an "L" at the center. By mistake, the plate was decorated exactly like the sample. *(Courtesy: The U.S. State Department. On loan from Philip J. Richmond)*

This orange Fitzhugh plate bears the initials "GS" for Gideon Swain, who had Nantucket connections. *(Courtesy: Nantucket Historical Association)*

The intertwined initials "CJB" identify this Rose Medallion service which originally belonged to Charles Joseph Bonaparte (1851–1921), grandson of Napoleon's brother Jerome Bonaparte who married Elizabeth Patterson of Baltimore. Charles Joseph was a dedicated lawyer and public servant in Baltimore and later served the nation as Secretary of the Navy in 1905 and Attorney-General until 1909 in Theodore Roosevelt's administration. The dinner service dates from about 1875.

This hot water oval covered platter is ornamented with early (circa 1825) and fine quality Rose Medallion decoration with plenty of gold in the background. The panels are outlined with a simple line and are generally melon shaped, with a definite leaf design at the top. Later Rose Medallion has ovoid panels outlined by a series of crescent squiggles. The monogram "A" is of gothic style which was popular on silver articles, too, during the mid-nineteenth century period. *(Courtesy: Herbert Schiffer Antiques)*

This Rose Medallion decoration is later than the preceeding, with crescent squiggles outlining the panels. The initial "C" stands for the original owners, members of the Cotting family of Salem, Massachusetts. *(Courtesy: The Peabody Museum of Salem)*

Silas H. Shringham was the flag officer in command of the United States *Cumberland* during bombardments of Forts Hatteras and Clark on the 28th and 29th of August, 1864. His initials "SHS" are on the rim of these Rose Medallion dishes with early "melon" shaped panels, circa 1825.

Another Mandarin decoration ornaments a set of dishes with the initial "T" on the rim which was made for the family of Isaiah Thomas, printer and founder, in 1812, of the American Antiquarian Society in Worcester, Massachusetts. Each plate has a different central scene of Chinese figures in room interiors and landscapes. *(Courtesy: The Peabody Museum of Salem)*

This distinctive monogram decoration with the stern of the ship *Arab*, has been found on only a few pieces of porcelain: three toddy jars and a cup. Two of the toddy jars are in the Winterthur collection with initials "JM". One toddy jar is in Mr. Feller's collection with initials "EHM", and a cup at the New Haven Colony Historical Society has slightly different overall decoration and initials "EJ". All three toddy jars incorporate the figure of Hope in a shield to the right, and an unknown European landscape with cart and horse on the opposite side. The cup lacks the figure of Hope and has an added bird resting on the urn above the initials. The details can be compared and seen to be varied.

None of these pieces has been accompanied by definite family associations, although the Beech family of Farmington, Connecticut has been suggested for the Winterthur jars.[57] *(Courtesy: top - The Henry Francis duPont Winterthur Museum; lower left - John Quentin Feller; lower right - The New Haven Colony Historical Society)*

The mourning of the death of George Washington was an extremely popular decorative theme in the first few years of the nineteenth century. The tomb, funerary urn, weeping willow tree and eagle were widely used devices which also appear on this Chinese porcelain service. Each piece also bears the initials of Washington's nephew J. Lewis and wife, apparently for whom it was made.[58] Plate 7″ diameter, syllabub 3¼″ high, platter 11 7/8 long, 4 5/8″ wide. *(Courtesy: The Henry Francis du Pont Winterthur Museum).*

The shield bears the monogram "J" below a closed helmet, traditionally indicating an esquire in English heraldry. This emblem was chosen for this dinner service which belonged to Thomas Jefferson, third President of the United States, who was a lawyer (esquire) by profession. Jefferson (1743–1826) was enamored of Chinese culture as evidenced by his 1770 design for a Chinese pavilion at Monticello.[59]

The underglaze blue border with hatching and dagger band is typical of the late eighteenth century style. *(Courtesy: The U. S. Department of State, lent by Thomas Jefferson Coolidge)*

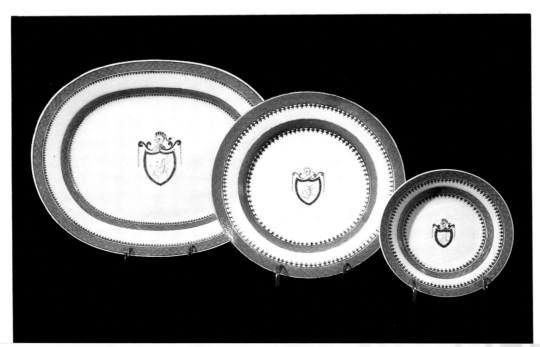

Gold initials JJ on this dinner service stand for the original owner John Jay (1745–1829) of New York. Jay's illustrious career as a public servant included some of the highest offices of government. In the new government, became secretary of foreign affairs and the first Chief Justice of the United States. While in this office he negotiated Jay's Treaty of 1795 settling many commercial trade grievances with Great Britain. That year he was also elected Governor of New York.

The porcelain is decorated simply with floral sprigs and gold details in the edge band. This service dates from about 1810. *(Courtesy: John Jay Homestead, New York State Parks and Recreation)*

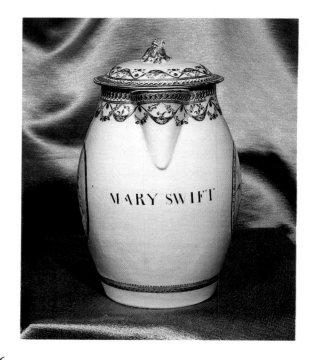

The purser of *The Empress of China* on her first trip to Canton was John White Swift of Philadelphia. He was unmarried, but had a sister and a sister-in-law both named Mary. His brother Charles married Mary Riche on December 31, 1783, just two months before the *Empress* sailed for Canton on February 22, 1784. This toddy jug was probably made as a wedding present for the couple. The eagle decoration is painted with fine detail, showing a Type XI eagle (see page 123) with American flag. Surrounding the eagle is a most appropriate inscription for this period of American commerce, "By virtue and valour we have freed our country, extended our commerce, and laid the foundation of a great empire." Opposite the eagle panel is the painting of a ship, probably copied from the *Hall* engraving (see page 153). Between these panels the jug is inscribed "Mary Swift." The jug probably traveled on the return leg of the *Empress* voyage to arrive in New York on May 11, 1785. *(Courtesy: Fred B. Nadler Antiques, Inc.)*

This large, 16-inch diameter, punch bowl was made circa 1800—1810 and given by a grateful ship's captain to the Bank of New Haven, Connecticut, which presumably helped to finance the trading voyage. It is still owned by the bank which is now called The First New Haven National Bank. The decoration consists of two inscriptions "Bank of New Haven" and two well drawn versions of the Type III eagle. *(Courtesy: The New Haven Colony Historical Society).*

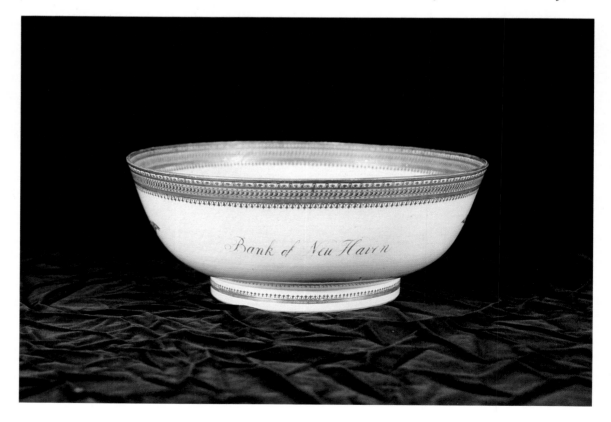

The Fitzhugh decoration on these oval platters contrast both in color and quality of decoration. The green is less refined over all than the orange and probably dates forty years later. The orange platter has a Type VI eagle (see page 118) and dates circa 1800, while the green platter has a Type VII eagle (see page 119), initials JLH, and dates circa 1840. The original owners for both are unknown.

99

The monogram M on the shield of the Type VI eagle (see page 118) indicates an unknown American owner. The green Fitzhugh decoration is representative of mid-nineteenth century painting. *(Courtesy: Fred B. Nadler Antiques, Inc.)*

Each of these forms is from a different sepia eagle tea service. The rim borders and eagle designs vary significantly; the tea caddy and open bowl are Type XI eagle (page 123) and the tea pot and sugar bowl are Type XII eagle, page 125. All date from the period circa 1800–1820. *(Courtesy: Henry Ford Museum and Greenfield Village)*

Constant Freeman owned the tea service from which this spoon tray comes with polychrome enamel type one Order of the Cincinnati decoration, see page 133–4. *(Courtesy: John Quentin Feller)*

A group of American market porcelain rests in front of a contemporary oil painting of Mount Vernon. The small dish has a central oval painted with another Mount Vernon scene (see page 168) and initials ABL for a member of the Virginia Lee family. The punch bowl has blue eagle decoration. The large plate is from George Washington's Society of the Cincinnati service with *Fame*, (see page 134). *(Courtesy: Samuel L. Lowe, Jr.)*

These dishes all were used by the Chew family at Cliveden near Philadelphia. They represent both mass produced and special order services of the mid-nineteenth century. From left, Canton, Fitzhugh, Rose Medallion, monogrammed C, classical figures. *(Courtesy: Cliveden, property of the National Trust for Historic Preservation)*

This group of Chinese porcelain dishes are decorated with some of the mass-produced designs which sold in the open market in America. From left, orange bird and sacred flower, green dragon, orange dragon, cabbage leaf, carp and crayfish, and green bird and sacred flower. All date from the mid-nineteenth century. *(Courtesy: Private Collection)*

The decoration on this punch bowl is symbolic for the Masonic order for which it was made at Hiram Lodge, Order of Freemasons in New Haven. (see page 142). *(Courtesy: The New Haven Colony Historical Society)*

Mass-produced porcelain was made in many variations such as these: *top row,* figures with bird and floral rim, eight Immortals surrounded by floral rim; *lower row,* cabbage, butterfly, figures with butterfly rim, Rose Canton, and floral.

Available on the open market, porcelain with these decorations became available to a widely diverse, eager American public. These patterns are, from left, Mandarin panels with floral groups, blue dragon, Mandarin, and Rose Medallion. The forms are interesting varieties of Chinese shapes.

John (1735–1826) and Abigail (1744–1818) Adams used the dinner service from which this plate comes at their home in Quincy, Massachusetts. He was the notorious and fascinating second President of the United States and she was his able and supporting partner throughout his dynamic political career. Another Chinese dinner service of these Adamses is shown with their monogram on page 67.

The single large floral decoration is highly unusual, and perhaps unique, among Chinese porcelain services, probably indicating this as a special order. There are so many connections between these people and merchants of the China trade that speculation of the service's origin must await factual evidence of the period. The gold edge band, daggar border and floral garland are all typical motifs of the mid-eighteenth century wares exported from Canton. This service may well date from the pre-Revolutionary period. *(Courtesy: The White House)*

George Washington's mother, Mary Ball Washington, (1708–1789), bequeathed this dinner service of raspberry Fitzhugh porcelain to her daughter. The decoration is of the most detailed type of the last quarter of the eighteenth century. *(Courtesy: Thomas D. and Constance R. Williams)*

The variety of color in which the Fitzhugh pattern was made creates an interesting comparison. The most common was blue, then orange, green, sepia, raspberry, yellow, black, and gold. The plate with combination sepia and green decoration was made for the Cadwalader family of Philadelphia. Monograms or crests were sometimes added to Fitzhugh decoration such as on pages 56, 61, 84–87. *(Courtesy: Fred B. Nadler Antiques, Inc.)*

Eagle decorations

The following group of porcelain objects are arranged by their eagle decorations into fifteen distinct types. Considering only the eagle emblems, and not the borders or initials, they form a progression from the most similar to the official seal of the United States, as it was designed in 1782, to interpretations by Chinese artists who had never seen an eagle.

The chart presents the details which define each type of eagle decoration. In each decoration the eagle clutches an olive branch of peace in the right talon and arrows of war in the left talon, except as noted. The eagles look toward the right and laurel branch, except as noted. In their order of presentation, the varying details are:

eagle, with wings outstretched

ribbon, held up above the eagle's chest, inscribed "E Pluribus Unum" (out of many, one)

shield, containing a blue shield with stars (often omitted) over alternating red and white vertical stripes. In only the first type is the shield bulged at the lower right and left corners and pointed at the middle with a straight top. In all subsequent types the shield is spade-shaped with a lower point and three points at the top

stripes, in the shield representing the blue field over red and white vertical stripes

crest, on the back of the eagle's head, appearing only in the first type

clouds, billowing in a circle or loosely around the eagle's head

stars, appearing within the circle of clouds or among loose clouds

half circle, tightly defined in an arc between an eagle's wings, often enclosing stars

ribbon, bending down over an eagle's chest and usually inscribed "E Pluribus Unum". The Fitzhugh decoration with eagle most commonly includes this type of ribbon

initials, within the shield

eagle, looking left rather than the customary right

ribbon, reading "In God We Hope", or a close variant

trumpet, clutched in the eagle's talons rather than the customary olive branch and arrows

109

anchor, covering right talons within an otherwise vacant shield

eagle, with wings arched down

Fame, included in association with an eagle

floral decoration in the shield

flags, replacing the olive branch and arrows, appearing only in the fifteenth type

bare branch, in right talon rather than the customary olive branch with leaves

EAGLE

Types:	Eagle, wings out	Ribbon - up	Shield	Stripes	Crest	Clouds - full	Stars	Half-circle	Ribbon - down	Initials	Eagle, right	Ribbon - Hope	Trumpet	Anchor	Eagle, wings down	Fame	Floral	Flags	Bare branch
I	X	X	X*	X	X	X	X												
II	X																		
III	X	X	X	X		X	X												
IV	X	X	X	X			X	X											
V	X		X			X	X		X	X									
VI	X		X						X	X									
VII	X		X	X					X										
VIII	X		X	X				X	X										
IX			X	X					X		X								
X	X		X									X	X	X					
XI			X	X				X							X				
XII			X					X		X					X				X
XIII			X					X		X					X	X			
XIV			X					X							X		X		X
XV			X					X							X		X	X	

*(official)

110

Type I Eagle

The official seal of the United States as it was adopted in 1782.

The eagle decoration on these dishes resembles the official Seal of the United States more closely than any other examples inspected by the authors to the time of this writing. Represented is the first official Seal of the United States as it was adopted in 1782.

The eagle is shown with outstretched wings and a ribbon flowing from his beak inscribed "E PLURIBUS UNUM". Upon his chest is the correctly shaped shield seen only in this set Type I eagle. Decorating the shield are horizontal and vertical stripes representing the blue field and red and white stripes of the United States flag. The eagle has feathers extending to a point behind his head, seen only on this set, Type I eagle. Above the bird is a full circle of clouds enclosing stars.

The porcelain service was made, probably in 1794, for Moses Brown (1738–1836) of Providence, Rhode Island. Moses was the youngest of four sons, his brothers Nicholas, John and Joseph each attaining their own fame. For a while between 1763 and 1773, he joined his brothers in the firm Nicholas Brown and Company. His wife's death in 1773 cast a depression over Moses who the following year, joined the Society of Friends (Quakers), freed his slaves and helped start the Rhode Island Abolition Society. His long, deep interest in cotton manufacturing then dominated his business interests. He brought over a master machinist from England and launched a successful factory. *(Courtesy: Mrs. Samuel Schwartz)*

111

The eagle on the Moses Brown service matches the eagle on a punch bowl made for Henry Smith, also of Providence, Rhode Island, who was supercargo on the ship *George Washington*. The ship was built in 1793, and sailed immediately for Canton. The Henry Smith punch bowl is inscribed on the inside "Henry Smith, Canton, 1794". It therefore seems logical to conclude that the Moses Brown service as well as this bowl were brought back to Providence aboard the *George Washington* on its return voyage in 1794.

This sixteen-inch diameter punch bowl is remarkable for the fine quality of its decoration as well as its date, owner's name, and history. Around the exterior the United States Seal is joined by a fouled anchor and motto "In God We Hope", by a painting of the ship *George Washington*, and by a mantled shield with the owner's initials "H. S." Therefore, the bowl serves to suggest a date period for each of these decorative motifs which are found singly on many other porcelain services. *(Courtesy, The Henry Francis du Pont Winterthur Museum).*

Type II Eagle

The second eagle decoration is a simple version of the United States Seal without a shield or ribbon. The eagle has outstretched wings and clutches the accustomed olive branch and arrows. *(Courtesy: The Henry Francis du Pont Winterthur Museum).*

The third eagle decoration displays the American eagle with outstretched wings supporting from his beak a ribbon inscribed "E PLURIBUS UNUM". The shield is spade shaped, as are each shield except in Type I eagles, decorated with horizontal and vertical stripes. The full clouds form a background around the eagle's head and enclose stars.

This platter has a border of peach-colored background and stylized leaf pattern popular especially around Philadelphia in the first quarter of the nineteenth century. *(Courtesy: Matthew and Elisabeth Sharpe).*

Type IV Eagle

This flagon and mugs from two different services have clearly painted Type IV eagle decoration. The eagle with outstretched wings holds a ribbon in its beak inscribed "E PLURIBUS UNUM" and displays the spade-shaped shield with stripes. The stars behind the eagle's head are now enclosed by a half-circle of clouds which are contained between the eagle's wings.

The flagon has a deep hatched blue border, with Nanking type dagger edge. The mugs, however, have the same eagle but a blue band punctuated with gold dots and a scalloped edge with dots. *(Courtesy: The Henry Francis du Pont Winterthur Museum).*

116

The fifth type of eagle decoration has the eagle with outstretched wings and spade-shaped shield as before, but here the ribbon flies down over his chest with the inscription "E PLURIBUS UNUM", the full clouds are loosely arranged between the wings with stars among them, and the shield bears the initials of the original owner.

In this example, the initials are JHRH within a rim border which resembles the floral pattern of chintz fabrics of the early nineteenth century. *(Courtesy: Mrs. Samuel Schwartz).*

The eagles on Fitzhugh porcelain are usually Type VI or Type VII eagles.

The sixth type of eagle has outstretched wings, a spade-shaped shield, and a ribbon flowing down across his chest. The shield supports one or more initials. There are no stars or clouds above or around the eagle's head.

In this example with sepia eagle the initials BSP are those of an unknown owner and the Fitzhugh decoration is painted in orange. Other Fitzhugh eagle services with initials were made in various colors, such as a sepia service for "BA" and a blue service for a family "M", both represented in the collection at the Henry Francis du Pont Winterthur Museum. *(Courtesy: The White House, Lent by The Honourable Peter Frelingheusen, Jr.).*

Type VII Eagle

The seventh type of eagle usually appears with Fitzhugh decoration and is similar to the sixth type of eagle except that the shield is painted with a blue field above red and white stripes. In this example the Fitzhugh decoration is painted in orange. *(Courtesy: Anonymous)*

The eighth type of eagle decoration has outstretched wings and a shield with horizontal and vertical stripes. The ribbon inscribed "E PLURIBUS UNUM" flows down across the eagle's chest. The stars above the eagle's head are enclosed by a half circle of clouds bounded by the eagle's wings. This example of the Type VIII eagle appears on a bowl with blue edge band and gold stars, typical of the 1810–1820 period. *(Courtesy: Matthew and Elisabeth Sharpe).*

Type VIII Eagle

Type IX Eagle

The ninth type of eagle looks to his left, rather than the customary right, and rests on an elaborate arrangement of trophies of war including flags, cannon, axe, wheel, cannon balls and tools. There are no arrows or olive branch clutched in the eagle's talons. The eagle has outstretched wings and displays a spade-shaped shield with horizontal and vertical stripes. The ribbon is flowing down across his chest, with lettering, in this example, "E RLUPIB UNUM".

This example of the ninth type of eagle is also noteworthy because the garniture jars have a loosely painted band of grape leaves and bunches of grapes which recall the fine borders of this design of the early nineteenth century. The use of trophies of war also appears in John Trumbull's 1820 painting of the Declaration of Independence (See chapter on Political Subjects) which was engraved and lithographed through the mid-19th Century. Therefore, this example probably dates from the mid-19th Century period.

A bowl with similar decoration belonged to Colonel Sylvanus Thayer (1785–1872), a commander of the U.S. Military Academy at West Point, New York and is now at the United States Department of State. *(Courtesy: The Henry Francis du Pont Winterthur Museum).*

Type X Eagle

The tenth style of eagle decoration has the eagle with outstretched wings, but there the similarity with the previous styles ends. This eagle clutches a shield in its right talons and a trumpet in its left talons. The shield is decorated with an anchor, the traditional emblem of Hope. A ribbon from the eagle's beak laces behind the shield and over the trumpet with the inscription "In God We Hope". Gold stars curl in a line above the eagle's head.

There are several sets of Chinese porcelain bearing this type of eagle decoration, three of them are shown here.

The punch bowl with wide floral exterior border is from a set of porcelain which belonged to John Jay, American Secretary of Foreign Affairs between 1784 and 1790, and colorful figure in the early years of the nation. There are three such eagles on this bowl. *(Courtesy: United States Department of State, Gift of Mrs. George P. Morse).*

This set of porcelain dinnerware with the style ten eagle decoration has a single gold band at its edge, a variation from the John Jay service. Circa 1815. *(Courtesy: The Henry Francis du Pont Winterthur Museum).*

A third variation is shown next, being a loosely painted grape leaf, vine and bunch pattern in overglaze enamels which have worn off on some of the pieces of this service. The large plate has a diameter of 9½ inches. Circa 1815. *(Courtesy: The Henry Francis du Pont Winterthur Museum).*

The American eagle decoration of the eleventh type has downturned wings which are found again on each of the remaining four types. These eagles form a circular overall design consistent with other decorations, especially of the early-to-mid-nineteenth century period, which are enclosed in round medallions[60]

The type eleven eagle supports a shield with stripes, and the clouds above the eagle's head are contained in an arc and have stars dotted within. Some of the type eleven eagles inspected had a bare branch in the talons, while others had the more common detail of leaves on the olive branch. Circa 1820, 6″ diameter. *(Courtesy: Matthew and Elisabeth Sharpe).*

The pistol-handled urn with cover has a variation of the eleventh type of eagle decoration. This is the only example inspected which has a ribbon in the eagle's beak, and downturned wings. There may be further examples of the design, or other variations of this type of eagle. The ribbon is inscribed "E Pluribus Unum" on the left side of the eagle's head. In this example, a further variation exists in the placement of the eagle in the upper portion of an oval to accommodate initials of the original owner, JES, who has not been identified. The wide gilded band around the oval and neck of the urn relates to other sets of this period, such as the Commodore Dale service with an urn, and the pair of pistol-handled urns with Chinese landscape and pagoda decoration, both shown in this book. *(Courtesy: Museum of the City of New York, Gift of Miss M. Remsen).*

opposite lower

The tea cup and saucer represent a miniature tea service made for an unknown American child. The eagle decoration is of the eleventh type, but painted in possibly a unique, free style. The border decoration is of poor quality grape vine design, probably indicating a late nineteenth century date. *(Courtesy: Peabody Museum of Salem)*

Type XII Eagle

The twelfth type of eagle decoration has a monogram of the original owner on the shield, and otherwise the same design as the eleventh type. The eagle has downturned wings, a shield, clouds, and stars in an arc between the wings.

The initials on this example are "IH" for the original owner Commodore Isaac Hull (1773–1843) who commanded the United States ship *Constitution*, popularly called *Old Ironsides*, during the War of 1812. *(Courtesy: The Mariners Museum, Newport News, Virginia)*

The entwined garlands on this border are among the most ornate found on examples of type twelve eagle decoration. The olive branch has no leaves in this example. Circa 1820. *(Courtesy: The Henry Francis du Pont Winterthur Museum)*

125

The twelfth type of eagle appears on several services with varying border decoration. The simple gold band on this example is one of the plainest borders inspected. There are no leaves on the olive branch here. *(Courtesy: Elinor Gordon).*

These two porcelain pieces come from separate tea services owned by the brothers Edward and Benjamin Cox of Salem, Massachusetts. The eagle decoration is of the twelfth type. *(Courtesy: Peabody Museum of Salem)*

The two tea caddies each display a variation of the twelfth type of eagle decoration significant enough to put them in a type of their own. The variation is the inclusion of the traditional personification of *FAME* in the form of a winged cherub with trumpet pointing to the eagle decoration with monogram. This is the thirteenth type of eagle decoration.

The example on the right has dark blue bands, wings on *FAME*, and eagle with the initials NEA, who has not been identified. The example on the left is painted with gold edge band and sepia figures with the initials D. L., so far unidentified. Early nineteenth century. *(Courtesy: The Henry Francis du Pont Winterthur Museum).*

The fourteenth type of eagle decoration has floral decoration in the shield, otherwise being the same as the eagles of types twelve and thirteen. The wings are turned down, stars and clouds are contained in an arc between the eagle's wings, and in this example the olive branch lacks leaves. Variations occur among the floral designs on different services, as well as a wide range of borders. On this example, the border is probably derived from a European ceramic design such as the English or French factories which were competing for business with the Chinese in the mid-nineteenth century. *(Anonymous)*.

The sepia and gold border variation on this coffeepot with type fourteen eagle decoration is a copy of the design popularized by the English firm Wedgwood in pattern books of the 1812 to 1822 period. The floral decoration on the shield is slightly different from the former and the following examples. The olive branch has no leaves. Circa 1825. 9¼" high. *(Courtesy: Matthew and Elisabeth Sharpe).*

128

Type XV Eagle

The type fourteen eagle decoration on this bowl has a distinctly different arc between the eagle's wings, a variant floral design on the shield, and a stylized border decoration popular in the United States around 1825. This eagle is also painted in a dark tone of blue rarely seen. *(Anonymous)*.

The fifteenth, and last, type of eagle decoration appears on this plate. Here the customary olive branch and arrows clutched in the eagle's talons are replaced with two flags, the American on the right side as we see it, and the Chinese on the left. Otherwise, the decoration is like the fourteenth type. The eagle with turned-down wings has a shield with floral decoration and stars and clouds in an arc between the wings. In this decoration the symbolic emblems of Chinese-American trade in porcelain are visually displayed.

The border decoration is copied from a European floral design source quite typical of the mid-to-late nineteenth century. Similar borders of the period appear on English, French, and German porcelain. 9 3/4″ diameter. Circa 1830. *(Courtesy: The Henry Francis du Pont Winterthur Museum)*.

129

The Society of the Cincinnati is a perpetual body composed of lineal male descendants of commissioned officers who served in the regular (Continental) American Army or Navy during the Revolution, 1775—1783.

It was established in 1783 by a group of officers who had served with Washington through the Revolution. The first proposal for the formation of the group was made April 15, 1783 by General Henry Knox. He foresaw a fraternal organization of the officers who were about to be demobilized. Within a month the officers at the New Windsor Cantonment on the west bank of the Hudson River had written a charter and sent it to each of the original thirteen states for approval. By the end of the year, each state had agreed with the charter and formed a State Society. In 1784, a fourteenth Society was formed in France for the eligible French officers. George Washington served as the Society's first President for sixteen years until his death in 1799. Alexander Hamilton was the second president for five years. About twenty-four hundred officers joined the Society as original members.

The name of the Society was derived from a Roman military officer Lucius Quinctius Cincinnatus, who twice was called upon by the Roman Senate to leave farming to become Dictator and put down civil disturbances. The founders of the Society saw a parallel in the lives of Cincinnatus and George Washington at a time when they, too, were about to put aside the sword and return to their lives as private citizens.

The medallion of the Society depicts Cincinnatus meeting the Senators at his plough. The badge of membership was designed by Major Pierre Charles L'Enfant. He selected the colors blue and white to symbolize the association between America and France. Badges have been made with various interpretations of L'Enfant's design, some with enameled details, others jeweled. The badge shown here belonged to Ralph Bart Bowles in 1783. It displays a gold bald eagle with white enameled head and tail. The body is formed by an oval seal decorated on one side with three gold human figures against a blue and green enamel background. These represent Cincinnatus receiving a sword from the Senators. The rim on this side is inscribed "Omnia Relinqt. Servare Rempub." On the reverse side a single figure (Cincinnatus) appears with a plow, rising sun on the left and towers on the right. The rim here is enameled with the inscription, "Virt. Praem. Soci. Cin. Ram. Inst. A. D. 1783." The head of the eagle is encircled by a green enameled laurel wreath. The medal is suspended from a wide blue ribbon edged with white. *(Courtesy: The Henry Francis duPont Winterthur Museum)*

Society of the Cincinnati membership certificate for James McClure dated 31 October, 1785.

Certain members of this patriotic Society had the emblem of the Society reproduced on Chinese porcelain tableware for their personal use. The primary example is the punch bowl decorated with an exact duplication in paint of the certificate of membership for Richard Varick (1753–1831). The certificate is dated January 1, 1784. Coincidentally on the same date he received a letter from George Washington thanking him for his competent work recording Washington's correspondance in forty volumes. Varick had been Washington's recording secretary to arrange, classify and copy all the correspondance and records of the headquarters of the Continental Army from 1781 through 1783.[61] Varick was president of the New York Society of the Cincinnati from 1806 until his death in 1831. The bowl was presumably made some time during his Presidency. It was given to its present owner in 1888. It is eighteen inches in diameter. *(Courtesy: The Washington Association of New Jersey)*

Besides the Varick bowl, eleven sets of porcelain dishes, with the emblem of the Society of the Cincinnati, are known to have been made. These can be divided into four different types of Cincinnati decoration. The first type resembles the badge, front and back. The second type has the addition of a figure of Fame holding the badge. The third type has two fames holding the badge, and the fourth type is a simplified version of the first type showing just the badge.

Captain Samuel Shaw (1754–1794) of Boston was an aid-de-camp of the Society's organizer General Henry Knox, supercargo of the *Empress of China* on its initial, 1784, voyage from New York to Canton, and later the American consul there.

Shaw recorded in his personal journal from Canton, "I wished to have something emblematic of the Order of the Cincinnati executed upon a set of porcelain. My idea was to have the American Cincinnatus, under the conduct of Minerva, regarding Fame, who, having received from them the emblem of the order, was proclaiming it to the world."[62]

Presumably Shaw then ordered porcelain services to be decorated. These may have been the type with the badge alone, with one Fame, with two Fames, all or some. Evidently, at least some of the porcelain so decorated was brought to America by the *Pallas* which arrived in Baltimore in August, 1785.

On August 12, 1785, the Baltimore <u>Advertiser</u> announced the arrival of the *Pallas* from Canton with goods to be sold at auction on the first of October. The list of porcelains offered at this sale included "Evening blue and white stone china cups and saucers; ditto painted; ditto with the arms of the Order of Cincinnati."[63] Five days later George Washington wrote to Colonel Tench Tilghman from Mount Vernon, that he wanted "...* a sett of large blue and white china dishes say a half a dozen more or less * one dozen small bowls blue and white * six wash hand guglets and basons...* with the badge of the Society of the Cincinnati if to be had."[64]

Porcelain services of the first type of Cincinnati decoration are known to have been made for six early members of the Society. In most cases, the original owners' initials can be found under the badge insignia. Samuel Shaw is the best documented owner of this type of porcelain. His service has his initials "SS" below the badge. Records have not confirmed when this and the other services of this type were actually imported, but it seems reasonable to think of them being ordered at

one time and delivered in time for the *Pallas* of Baltimore (1785) or *Empress of China* (1786) on its second trip to New York to have brought them to America. Besides Shaw's service, the others were made for five other Massachusetts residents: General Henry Knox (1750–1806) of Boston, secretary of the Society; William Eustis; Dr. David S. Townsend of Boston; Benjamin Lincoln (1733–1810) of Hingham; and Constant Freeman of Charleston. *(Courtesy: The Henry Francis duPont Winterthur Museum)*

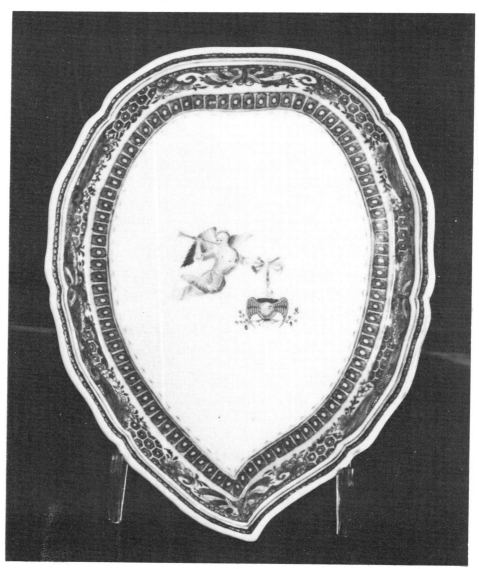

Examples of the second type of Cincinnati porcelain with the figure of fame holding the badge has descended in three families, probably indicating at least three separate services originally. George Washington (1732–1799) apparently acquired one service some time after his request in August of 1785 to Tench Tilghman to obtain such porcelain for him. The leaf shaped plate shown here is from the Washington set with full traditional documentation. Another set has descended in the family of Henry (Light Horse Harry) Lee (1756–1818) of Virginia, and pieces of an apparent third service with unknown origins have appeared. *(Courtesy: The White House)*

The simple version of the Cincinnati badge shown on this tea caddy may be a later interpretation of the decorations seen previously. The overall quality is less refined and the detail is limited here. The service was originally made for Richard Humpton of the Pennsylvania second regiment. *(Courtesy: The United States Department of State, lent by the Lucile and Robert H. Gries Charity Fund)*

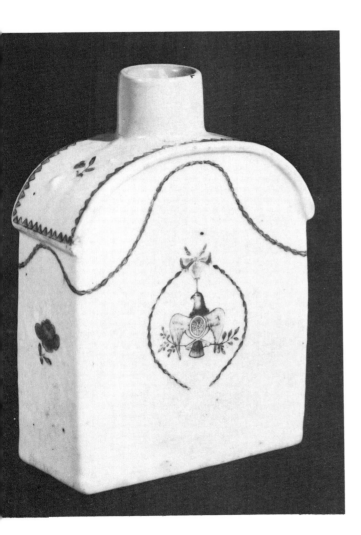
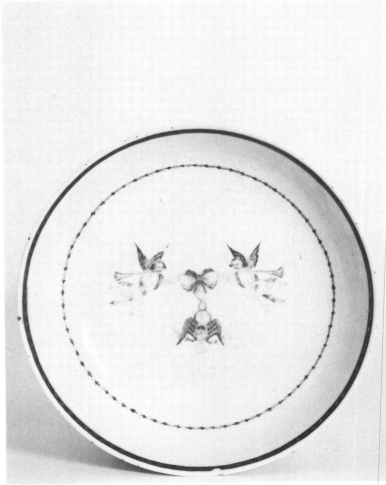

Twin figures of Fame support the Cincinnati badge on this third type of porcelain decoration. This service was originally owned by Doctor/Congressman/Massachusetts governor William Eustis (1753–1825) making him the only owner of two Cincinnati services, for he is known to have also owned one of the first type. He was vice-president of the Society of the Cincinnati from 1786 to 1870 and again in 1820. *(Courtesy: The Henry Francis duPont Winterthur Museum)*

With a Society of the Cincinnati badge decoration similar to the Richard Humpton service, this punch bowl gains added interest because of its central decoration. The portrait of George Washington is most probably a copy of a print, possibly by Amos Doolittle.[65] Surrounding the portrait is a chain of thirteen rings, each inscribed with the name of an original state. This chain may be a derivation of the Martha Washington service shown on page 95. One may speculate that the bowl was made after its prototype designs as a composit of them. *(Courtesy: The Historical Society of Pennsylvania)*

Masonic & Political decorations

Decorated with polychrome Masonic emblems, this bowl was made about 1790 for Adam Eckfeldt. Initials in a cartouche on the side are "A. M. E." He worked at the Philadelphia Mint from 1795 to 1839 when he retired as chief coiner.[66] *(Courtesy: Philadelphia Museum of Art, gift of Henry Cowell DuBois)*

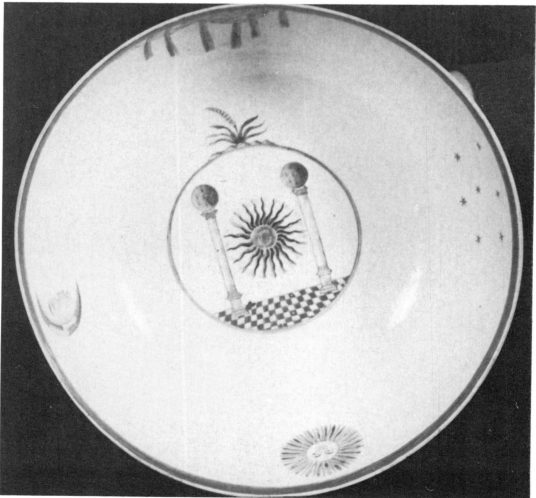

Varied Masonic emblems form the decorative design for these pieces circa 1790–1810. *(Anonymous)*

(Courtesy: Matthew and Elisabeth Sharpe).

139

Some porcelain with Masonic emblems survives today from the large quantities exported from China in the 1790's and early 1800's. Here the border design is restrained with the gilt initials of the original owner enclosed by the Masonic emblem. *(Courtesy: Matthew and Elisabeth Sharpe)*.

Ornamented by a gilt grape leaf pattern border edge, this very complete tea service is decorated with the Masonic symbols of T-square and compass. The gilt script initials of the original owner also appear on some pieces in the set. Circa 1790–1810. *(Courtesy: Herbert Schiffer Antiques).*

The small rectangular tray has Masonic emblems and a shield with the monogram "RCC", of the original owner. Circa 1800. 6¼". (*Courtesy: John Quentin Feller*).

Originally purchased by Major William Munson in 1800, the bowl was brought back from China by Captain Nathaniel Green. It has been on loan to the New Haven Colony Historical Society from Hiram Lodge, Order of Freemasons, since 1893. Circa 1800–1820. (*Courtesy: New Haven Colony Historical Society*).

Political topics are a scarce subject for decoration on Chinese porcelain. The three political scenes which have American connections are joined by only a few others of English and European significance.

The "Wilkes and Liberty" bowl is similar to others with longstanding American connections decorated similarly but with the title "Arms of Liberty". The decoration consists of two caricature portraits of John Wilkes (1727–1797) and William Murray, Lord Mansfield (1708–1793), both probably copied from contemporary engravings of the 1770–80 period when the bowls are believed to have been made.

John Wilkes was an English politician of liberal persuasion whose fiery career included being expelled and re-elected to Parliament five times. He violently supported liberal causes and became a friend of the American effort for Revolution.

William Murray rose through political ranks to the office of Lord Chief Justice from 1756 to 1788. He violently opposed Wilkes' actions and re-elections so became the target in this decoration for the attack on the established government.

The decoration carries out their opposition. The motto across the lower ribbon "Always ready in a good cause" rests below Wilkes' likeness. Two garlands (of victory) surround Wilkes in the cartouche with the supporters being the traditional figure of Liberty, and Wilkes standing with sash. The crest of a (victorious) *lion passant argent* surmounts the cartouche.

Mansfield's portrait with long hair has the motto "Justice sans pitie" on a ribbon below the cartouche. Here chains (of oppression) flank the portrait with supporting figures of The Devil and Lord Mansfield standing with sash. The green serpent crest above this portrait is a further symbol of evil, being lowly and trodden upon (by the lion opposite). The titles "Wilkes and Liberty" on this, and "Arms of Liberty" on others appear over Wilkes' portrait only. *(Courtesy: The White House, lent by the Lucile and Robert H. Gries Foundation).*

(Courtesy: The Henry Francis duPont Winterthur Museum)

(Courtesy: The Henry Francis duPont Winterthur Museum)

(Courtesy: The Henry Francis duPont Winterthur Museum)

146

(Courtesy: The Henry Francis duPont Winterthur Museum)

In the last example, the figures not only have Oriental expressions, but are dressed in Oriental clothing and the room has taken on Oriental features. The eagle here is moved above the scene. *(Courtesy: The Henry Francis du Pont Winterthur Museum.)*

147

The Currier and Ives print "Surrender of General Burgoyne at Saratoga, N.Y., Oct. 17th, 1777."
(Courtesy: Kenneth M. Newman, Old Print Shop, New York City)

On October 17, 1777 British Lieutenant-General John Burgoyne surrendered his troops to American Major-General Horatio Gates at Saratoga, New York.[69]

As on the preceding Declaration of Independence porcelain, the decoration on this punch bowl probably derives from a painting (1817–21) by John Trumbull through a later print. Since Colonel John Trumbull served Washington during the Revolution and made a map of the 1777 encounters at Ticonderoga,[70] his interest in the events was personal.

In the painting Burgoyne is shown offering his sword to Gates with General Daniel Morgan in white and former General Philip J. Schuyler in civilian dress to the right. General Gates returned Burgoyne's sword, and invited him to dine in his tent.

Trumbull's painting was copied by O. Knirsch on stone for a lithograph published in 1852 by Nicholas Currier, later of the New York firm Currier and Ives. This print may be the design source for this bowl. The major characters are similarly placed in the landscape with the tent and American flag to the right. However, here

148

no sword is being exchanged. There are no epaulettes on the British officers, the principal men are holding hands, and the figures on each side are joined by mustached men in the background. Like the Declaration porcelain, the American eagle is flying above, but here the banner reads "The Surrender of Burgoyne," as begins the title on the Currier print. *(Courtesy: The White House, gift of Mrs. Jeannette Robinson Marks)*

Napoleon Bonaparte's oldest brother Joseph Bonaparte owned these urns when he lived at Point Breeze, Bordentown, New Jersey during exile from France between 1815 and 1840. Another brother, Jerome, married Elizabeth Patterson of Baltimore while exiled in America, and from them stems the Bonaparte family in in America. These urns typify the family's interest in classical formalism of the late 19th Century in America, and the Bonaparte family's personal identification with the ancient monarchies, to whom they made frequent comparisons.[71]
(Courtesy: The Henry Francis du Pont Winterthur Museum).

Benjamin Chew Wilcocks (1776–1845) of Philadelphia was for a period in the early 19th Century the American Consul at Canton and had a home in Macao between 1800 and 1829. Some time during this period he ordered toddy jugs made for himself and a few friends.[72]

On these he had painted a portrait of George Washington in the same fashion as black transfer printed decorations on English Liverpool jugs of the period. The portrait is a painting after an engraving probably by David Edwin after Gilbert Stuart's portrait of 1795. The engraving was used as the frontispiece of the first published edition in 1796 of Washington's Farewell Address. A copy of this address could easily have been among the personal baggage of Wilcocks or any other American at Canton. The traditional story of this jug, and three or four others like it,[73] links them with Wilcocks originally and a nephew, Edward Tilghman of Philadelphia, who received one and whose initials "ET" appear on two. One jug was initialed "BCW" for Wilcocks.[74] *(Courtesy: The Henry Francis du Pont Winterthur Museum).*

151

There exist at least two items of Chinese porcelain with the likeness of Commodore Stephen Decatur, Senior (1751–1808) as decoration. A punch bowl is described in detail in an article published in 1937 in the magazine *Antiques*.[75] The toddy jar here has very different border and accompanying ornamentation, but exactly the same portrait of Commodore Decatur. The inspiration was most certainly a watch-paper-sized portrait by Saint Memin of Philadelphia which was in the possession of the Decatur family at the time of the 1937 article mentioned above. The toddy jar was probably made circa 1800.

Commodore Decatur Sr. of Philadelphia should not be confused with his also-famous son (1779–1820) by the same name. The father was a celebrated ship's captain who commanded the *USS Delaware* during one of the early battles of the war with France in 1798, which is the subject of additional decoration on the punch bowl mentioned above. *(Courtesy: The Henry Francis du Pont Winterthur Museum).*

Marine decorations

'Britannia's Glory first from SHIPS Arose –
To SHIPPING still her power & wealth she Owes
Let each Experienc'd BRITON then Impart
His Naval skill To Perfect naval Art.

Billings Sc.

The English ship *Hall* was engraved by Billings and used as the frontispiece for William A. Hutchinson's *A Treatise on Practical Seamanship* published in Liverpool in 1777 and 1791. This treatise apparently found its way to Chinese porcelain painters for by the time American ships were trading in Canton in 1784, pictures of Western ships on porcelain bore a striking resemblance to this engraving. Most of the early marine broadside views on Chinese porcelain are believed to be derived from this print. The joy comes in finding diversions from the design with regard to flags, pennants, sails, guns and rigging. *(Courtesy: The Library Company of Philadelphia).*

153

There are several Chinese porcelain punch bowls in existence decorated with reproductions of the English engraving of the ship *Hall* from Hutchinson's *Treatise,* shown on the previous page. They all date within a four year period. The first known member of this group was apparently made in 1785 and is inscribed *"Empress of China,* John Green, Commander." This is at the New Jersey State Museum (see the illustration following). Another is in the collection of the Peabody Museum of Salem, Massachusetts with full documentation of its history. This one shows the same ship identified as the "Ship *Grand Turk* at Canton 1786." One in the collection of the Philadelphia Maritime Museum has the initials "RD" for Richard Dale and was apparently brought to America in 1788.[76] Another was made for John Barry and the *Alliance* the same year and remains in a private collection.[77] Mention of a fifth is made in an article in *Antiques* magazine, December, 1937.[78] The location of this is unknown.

opposite, top

This very important bowl was made for Captain John Green, who was captain of *The Empress of China* on her first trip to the Orient in 1784–1785.

The outside is decorated with a Greek key band, polychrome floral swags around the top, polychrome bouquets and sprays of flowers on the sides, and green leaves around the base. The interior is decorated with a fish scale and tassel band around the top, and has a large picture of a ship flying an enormous American flag, in the interior of the bowl. Above the ship is a legend on a banner "John Green/ Empress of China/ Commander". This ship brought back 962 piculs = 128,234.6 lbs. of chinaware in 137 chests of china (averaging 936 lbs. each). This ship, the first American ship to China, was sent out by Robert Morris of Philadelphia and Daniel Parker & Co. of New York. Major Samuel Shaw went out as supercargo. The cost of the venture was $120,000, and the outward trip to Macao took six months. *(Courtesy: New Jersey State Museum).*

opposite, bottom

The *Grand Turk* bowl is particularly interesting of this group because it is specifically mentioned in the ship's log. This reference explains the significance of this particular bowl and probably each of the bowls with similar decoration. Mr. W. Vans, Jr., supercargo of the *Grand Turk,* and Captain E. West "had now completed their business with Pinqua (the Chinese Hong merchant), and were making their preparation to leave his factory at Canton. On the day of their departure, they went to make their farewell visit to the old merchant. Pinqua received them in his usual courteous manner and after the customary formality of tea drinking, he summoned his servants who brought in a large china bowl and placed it before his guests. To their surprise, they found it was beautifully decorated with a painting of the *Grand Turk* under full sail and bore the inscription, 'Ship *Grand Turk* at Canton, 1786.' Pinqua begged his visitors to accept this gift as a souvenir of their stay at Canton."[79]

The *Grand Turk* was owned by Elias Hasket Derby of Salem, Massachusetts. This was Derby's first venture to Canton and was so successful that he sent numerous ships in its wake throughout the first half of the nineteenth century. The punch bowl has a capacity of three gallons. *(Courtesy: The Peabody Museum of Salem)*

The *Neptune* with Captain Daniel Greene (1765–1817) of New Haven sailed from New York 1796–1799[0] and went to the Folkland Islands for 53,000 sealskins which were sold in Canton for tea, nankeens, silk and 150 boxes of china to be sold in Boston.[80] *(Anonymous)*

There were several ships named *Friendship* of Salem which could have inspired this decoration. It may be the *Friendship* owned by Joseph Peabody which was attacked and captured at sea near Sumatra in 1830.[81] It seems to have been made in the early nineteenth century, perhaps from an original design which is significantly different from other ship portraits. The border decoration of figures playing and floral vignettes in oval reserves may be a stock pattern. *(Courtesy: Peabody Museum).*[82]

The Union Line was started in 1813 as the first company operating steamers on the Chesapeake Bay. It was sold to the Pennsylvania Railroad in the early 1850's. In 1816, the Union Line built at Baltimore a two hundred and forty ton vessel named *Philadelphia* which ran the Philadelphia route from Baltimore to Frenchtown, Maryland. At Frenchtown, passengers boarded a stage, later a railroad car, for New Castle, Delaware where they met another boat for the last leg of the trip to Philadelphia. The *Philadelphia* was used until 1841.[83] *(Courtesy: The Henry Francis duPont Winterthur Museum)*

Unidentified ships flying the flag of the United States are found as decoration on a variety of Chinese porcelain forms. Most examples relate to tea services or other drinking vessels rather than serving dishes of a dinner set. The painting is usually not of the finest quality perhaps indicating that these pieces were made for the mass market rather than for individual orders. The engraving of the ship *Hall* may have served as the phototype for most of the American ship decorations, although variations in the designs occur frequently. There does not seem to be a progression of ship designs from early to late with reference to the border decorations; we can merely suggest a date around 1800 for the group.

(Courtesy: John Quentin Feller)

(Courtesy: Samuel L. Lowe, Jr.)

(Courtesy: Matthew and Elisabeth Sharpe)

(Courtesy: Herbert Schiffer Antiques, Inc.)

The poor quality of decoration on this plate, one of several known to exist with the same scene, may suggest a mid-to-late nineteenth century date. The incident which inspired the decoration, however, may have taken place earlier, perhaps during the War of 1812 era, when the American ship was boarded by the crew of an enemy ship. The crew is shown on deck, as if summoned to attention. A boarding party approaches from the left and smoke fills the central deck above the cannon level. The ship apparently has been hit. *(Courtesy: Peabody Museum of Salem, Edward and Louise duPont Crowninshield Collection)*

This ship decoration is unusual in that there is no water around the ship. *(Courtesy: John Quentin Feller)*

The War of 1812 provided events of national pride in the United States, some of which have been commemorated on porcelain from China. Naval encounters of this war were the most dramatic and decisive, and many were sketched, engraved, and distributed to the loyal public who boasted of their success. This flagon or toddy jug is decorated with two scenes of naval encounters of the War of 1812. On one side the action of October 25, 1812 between the American frigate *United States* with the British frigate *Macedonian* is pictured. On the reverse side the action of September 5, 1813 between the American Brig *Enterprise* with the British Brig *Boxer* is shown. Not shown here but between these scenes under the spout is a small painting of a sailor with a banner inscribed "Don't give up the ship", the famous American naval motto popularized at this period. Initials WC of the unknown original owner are below this painting. Circa 1815. *(Courtesy: The Henry Francis du Pont Winterthur Museum).*

163

The strength & Wealth of the Nation

International commerce became essential to the struggling business community of the United States after the American Revolution. Families used to the conveniences of life were strained to develop their own means of support anew in an infant nation. Therefore, the shipbuilding industry grew rapidly as commerce extended around the world.

One person apparently saw fit to commission a decoration for Chinese porcelain commemorating shipbuilding or a person related to it. This punch bowl bears a painting of a ship outlined by its ribs and supported by beams as it is under construction. "The strength and wealth of the nation" are proclaimed above the ship and on the reverse is an American eagle with American flag and badges of war. Clearly this bowl demonstrates pride in American naval power early in the nineteenth century when it was made.

A Chinese porcelain bowl with similar, though more sophisticated, painted decoration of a ship being built was presented to Henry Eckford, an American naval architect, by the Sultan of Turkey about 1830.[84] *(Courtesy: The Henry Francis du Pont Winterthur Museum).*

opposite:

The decoration on this flagon or toddy jar is painted in overglaze enamels in a rather freehand style. The design shows an unidentified American ship in calm seas on one side and in a raging rainstorm with turbulent seas on the reverse side. There are no initials or other inscription to aid in identifying the original owner. The gold decorated grapevine border around the top has appeared in this work on several other items of the first quarter of the nineteenth century. *(Courtesy: The Peabody Museum of Salem).*

Philadelphian Raphaelle Peale signed this oil on panel painting in the lower right corner and dated it 1822. The "Still Life with Strawberries" is a most engaging painting and intriguing to this study because the tea service is undoubtedly Chinese porcelain. The forms and border designs resemble many tea sets illustrated in this book. The sugar bowl's panel is painted with a most interesting marine view of a harbor with two ships anchored. In the foreground a boy or sailor and a dog flank a large anchor, and the boy appears to be holding string for (a kite of?) two geese. We shall always wonder if the saucers, bowl and pitcher were similarly decorated, for no piece is currently known with this decoration. Raphaelle Peale (1774–1825), oldest son of Charles Willson Peale (1741–1827), brother of Rembrandt, Titian and Rubens, and nephew of James Peale (1749–1831), was surrounded by painting from childhood. He is best known for his still life paintings. *(Photograph courtesy of Graham Gallery, Ltd.)*

Western landscape decorations

The Pennsylvania Hospital was organized in Philadelphia. About 1800, artist George I. Parkyns sketched the Pennsylvania Hospital building's facade on Pine Street. The hospital's Board of Managers forwarded the sketch to Philadelphia artist Benjamin West in London who had W. Cooke make an engraving of it. In about 1801, an engraving was taken to China where the bowl was made and decorated. The bowl was brought from Canton to Philadelphia on the ship *Dispatch* with William Redwood, Jr. as supercargo. Redwood's uncle Joseph Saunders Lewis, Treasurer of the Hospital, presented the bowl to the Board on April 26, 1802. Between 1873 and 1974 the bowl was in the possession of ancestors of the donor, and has once more been given to the Hospital.

The bowl has a capacity of three gallons of punch. The exterior has two small underglaze sepia landscape scenes, and two large overglaze enameled polychrome views of the Hospital. *(Courtesy: The Pennsylvania Hospital).*

167

The landscape decoration in oval panels on these porcelain dishes depicts George Washington's home in Virginia, Mount Vernon. The origin of the design was a painting of the country estate and house by William Birch done about 1800. In 1803 Samuel Seymour engraved the scene. The first example shown here is from a sepia service that also has the initials "SS" above the scene and in a shield, and is known to have belonged to the artist Samuel Seymour himself. Several finely painted examples in this book demonstrate the ability of Chinese artists to exactly duplicate their print sources. Therefore, it is reasonable to suppose that Seymour ordered his set of porcelain with a hastily drawn likeness of his engraving of Mount Vernon as the design source.

The five other examples with this decoration are arranged to show, first, a deterioration of the design of the Mount Vernon scene, and second, variations in border patterns which may also show a chronologic progression from about 1805 to about 1870. *(Courtesy: John Quentin Feller).*

The gold band and simple garland border decoration are typical of the first few years of the nineteenth century. 4 7/8". *(Courtesy: The Henry Francis du Pont Winterthur Museum).*

The draped garland border on this Mount Vernon plate is consistent with the Federal style popular circa 1810–20, the probable date of the plate's manufacture. *(Courtesy: Elinor Gordon)*

The Mount Vernon decoration is surrounded on this plate by an orange band and enameled overglaze garland. Mid-19th Century. *(Anonymous).*

This tea bowl with Mount Vernon decoration has a polychrome overglaze enamel band and dates from the 1820 period. 5 7/16″ diameter. *(Courtesy: Elinor Gordon)*

The Mount Vernon decoration on this tea bowl and saucer is a vague interpretation of the Seymour engraving or Birch painting probably made in the middle of the nineteenth century. The border decoration also suggests this date as it is a weak interpretation of the Fitzhugh pattern. *(Courtesy: Matthew and Elisabeth Sharpe).*

Miniature Chinese porcelain tea services are rarely found with their complete pieces. The polychrome decoration on this miniature service is probably derived from an engraving of European origin. The set has descended in the Morris family of Philadelphia but it is not definitely known to have been made specifically for one of their members. Similar services have survived in England. *(Courtesy: Matthew and Elisabeth Sharpe).*

Charming landscape scenes are found in Europe as well as America. This fishing scene of fine detail in sepia and gold has a history in Philadelphia although the original owner is unknown. The detail of the border decoration is unusually well painted dating the plate from the 1790—1810 period. 7 5/8" diameter. *(Courtesy:*

Several sets of dishes are known with this Quaker and cow decoration. The widely publicized story of the origin of the design in the Hollingsworth-Morris family[85] can be verified by notebooks which have been retained in the family. There are, however, sets of slightly varying decoration, and at least one with the initials of another family which suggest that either additional sets were made in China after the original, or that a design source other than a hand drawn picture is responsible for the decoration.

The design is of a cow with calf and a man, usually referred to as a Quaker, within a landscape with large tree to the left and sometimes a goat resting beneath the tree. A smaller tree is right of center, and sometimes a small house is in the right background. Some sets are painted in black, some in sepia, all in overglazed enamels.

The first example has black decoration, a goat beneath the large tree, and loosely arranged leaves on both trees with the small house to the right. *(Courtesy: Matthew and Elisabeth Sharpe)*.

The black overglaze enamel decoration on this Quaker and cow porcelain is joined by the initials WLD which stand for the original owner, W.L. Duane of the New York Duane family. The trees have loose leaves, the goat rests beneath the left tree, and the small houses appear at the right. *(Courtesy: John Quentin Feller)*.

The Quaker and cow decoration on these pieces from two different services are painted in sepia tones. On one service a gold band surrounds the rim, on the other the rim is plain. The leaves are tightly bunched into round groups. There is no goat beneath the left tree, and there are no houses on the right side. Considering the design alone, this decoration appears to be a later, Chinese interpretation of the two preceding sets. However, these are pieces which have descended in the Hollingsworth-Morris family with the story of their design originating in a drawing by Mary Hollingsworth-Morris. Perhaps all the information on this design has not yet been exposed, for these contradictions are apparent.

173

Doctor Benjamin Waterhouse (1754–1846) of Cambridge, Massachusetts, was a Professor at Harvard University and responsible for cowpox vaccination to fight smallpox in America. Doctor Edward Jenner (1749–1823) of London first proved that cowpox innoculation was effective against smallpox in 1796, although the technique had been known since the early seventeen hundreds. In 1800, Doctor Waterhouse innoculated his own children against smallpox and advertised his success through publications.[86]

Concurrent experimentation was going on in England where Doctor John Lettsom published his results in a small booklet *Observations on the Cowpox* in 1801.[87] (The title page is reproduced here)

To celebrate the success of the vaccinations, Doctor Waterhouse had made for him at Canton a porcelain tea service with cows as the main decoration. Waterhouse apparently furnished Lettsom's title page as a source for the decoration on his porcelain, for the likeness is remarkable.

A second decoration is found on the major pieces of Doctor Waterhouse's tea set. Here there are two cows painted below the initial "W." A specific source for this design is not known, yet the Chinese painters may have invented the scene themselves. *(Courtesy: Boston Medical Library)*

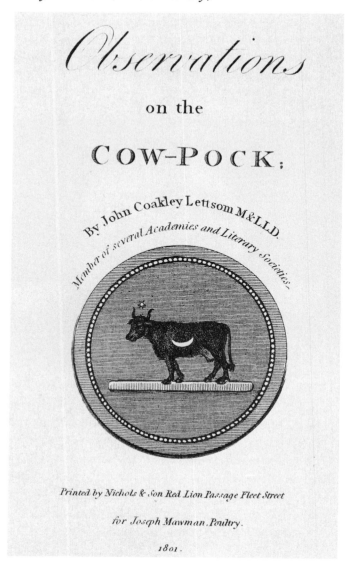

175

The sepia painted decoration on this set of plates depicts a complex landscape with three cows, two men fishing, swimming ducks, a covered bridge, a two-story house, a sailboat, and several varieties of trees. An engraving of the period circa 1800, probably inspired the design which has long been associated with the Bache family of Philadelphia. Several of the large summer residences in Philadelphia on the Schuylkill River can be suggested for this scene. *(Courtesy: Private Collection)*

opposite:

Rockland Mansion was built by George Thompson in 1810 on land overlooking the Schuylkill River in Philadelphia. After several owners in the intervening years, the house and twenty-six acres was sold to Isaac Cooper Jones in 1834 and remained in this family's posession until it was purchased by the city of Philadelphia in 1869. This miniature Chinese porcelain tea service has sepia and gold decoration showing a liberal view of Rockland and the initials "HEJ." The service was made after 1834 for Isaac C. Jones' daughter, Hanna Elizabeth Jones, who was born in 1812.

(Courtesy: John Quentin Feller)

177

Four animated figures in the central medallion are painted in polychrome on these dishes which have descended in the Guest family of the Philadelphia suburbs. John Guest (1768–1817) was a likely owner. The figures have been traditionally identified as Adam and Eve with Cane and Able. The use of a weeping willow tree and Roman clothing indicate an original date during the fervent classical period circa 1810. *(Courtesy: Private Collection)*

Unknown landscape decorations are found frequently on Chinese porcelain. These may have been stock patterns, for they are not always accompanied by initials. These few have strong American histories since the early nineteenth century when they were made. *(Courtesy : The Daughters of the American Revolution Museum, bequest of Katherine Scott Hills)*

(Courtesy: Herbert Schiffer Antiques, Inc.)

(Courtesy: John Quentin Feller)

179

(Courtesy: John Quentin Feller)

180

Chinese landscape decorations

Several series of Chinese watercolor paintings showing aspects of the tea, porcelain and yardgoods trade with Western merchants were brought to America during the early nineteenth century. The Winterthur and Peabody Museum of Salem collections each have some; those shown on this and the opposite pages are in private collections. Knowing the paintings, it should not seem surprising to find porcelain with similar decoration, yet these examples are scarce. This cup and saucer are decorated to show workmen packing tea in a merchant's shop in Canton.

Decoration on Chinese porcelain in the famille rose pallet of Chinese figures as the primary subject are known as Mandarin decoration and there are many variations found. Most of the fine quality Mandarin decoration has a great deal of gold in the background, detailed painting and floral, butterfly, bird and sometimes dragon figures in the borders. There are several Mandarin sets known to have been made for Americans. The primary example is the twenty inch diameter punch bowl brought back to Boston in 1832 by Commodore Matthew Dewey. A shield shaped panel on one side is inscribed with the full information about the bowl, making this one of the best documented American market bowls. The inscription reads, "From the Commander and Ward Room officers of the U. S. ship *Peacock* To Dwight Boyden, Tremont House, Boston, 1832."

Tremont House was a favorite bar and meeting place for merchants and sailors of the time; therefore, the gift of this punch bowl to the proprietor was especially appropriate. The decoration is painted with minute detail, helping to establish similar decorations within the first half of the nineteenth century. The interior bottom has an exquisite painting of the harbor at Canton. *(Courtesy: The Bostonian Society, Old State House)*

The Mandarin decoration on this covered vegetable dish is quite finely painted and all the more interesting because under the lid and on the base is the marking "SB 1842" in a circle.

Mandarin decoration is painted in polychrome enamels over the glaze with the major panel containing oriental people in a variety of activities. Sometimes shown indoors, often in a Chinese landscape, the figures are usually painted with precise detail and often with gold in the background or as highlights.

The date on this piece is appropriate for a date of manufacture. The initials have not been identified, but presumably represent the original owner. Most related forms with Mandarin decoration can be dated in the decade around 1842. This piece was found near Boston, Massachusetts. *(Courtesy: John Quentin Feller)*

A very beautiful dinner service is represented by this plate of Mandarin decoration with cornet and inscription "Exmo Sor Marques de Almendares." It was made for the Cuban Marquis de Almendares Ignacio Herrera who purchased this colonial title in 1842. Herrera was the great-grandson of Gonzalo Luis Herrera, fourth Marquis de Villalta and nephew of Gonzalo Jose de Herrera, conde of Fernandina, a grandee of Spain. Ignacio Herrera owned large coffee and sugar plantations, railroads and a textile mill. He probably ordered the dinner service soon after he became enobled. 9 ¾" diameter, circa 1845. (Courtesy: John Quentin Feller)

The Mandarin decoration on this hot water tureen and platter is joined by the Chinese happiness symbol in gold to the left of center on the lid's rim. This symbol can be found prominently on forms probably intended as special gifts, such as individual plates and important serving pieces, not necessarily on whole sets. This tureen has a tradition of ownership to President Ulysses S. Grant to whom it was probably a gift. (Courtesy: The Peabody Museum of Salem)

A variety of Chinese landscapes appear on porcelain decorated with the Rose Medallion pattern which combines floral panels with scenes of figures in rooms or landscapes. Rose Medallion services with monograms are shown on pages 89 to 91. Rose Medallion decoration is painted in polychrome enamels over the glaze with a round central Medallion containing a pink peony - the "Rose of China." The borders and floral areas have a lot of gold in the background on earlier and better quality services. The panels with people vary, some with a great deal of gold detail. Dinner services of Rose Medallion decoration were mass produced for export to the West in large numbers over the last five decades of the nineteenth century. A study of the variations in the panels is not in the scope of this book, but deserves careful consideration at another time. Here a sampling of the variety found will be noticed in the examples of the chapters on monogram and floral decoration.

Among the documented services of Rose Medallion in America is that made for Daniel Gould Fowle (1831–1891), governor of North Carolina from 1888 to 1891. The service of one hundred and ten pieces is marked "Made in China" in underglaze red. This mark was required by U. S. Customs law for imports by 1890. *(Courtesy: Herbert Schiffer Antiques)*

The Canton pattern of underglaze blue decoration was mass produced in Canton and widely imported to America throughout the mid-nineteenth century period. Large dinner services with serving pieces were imported for open sale. Numerous inventories of this period call for "Chinaware," "India China," and similar general terminology which can sometimes be interpreted to include Canton ware. The term Canton to identify this pattern seems to have grown out of frequent use in the twentieth century to the point that it now refers exclusively to the porcelain with dash (rain) and scalloped (cloud) border bands inside the blue edge. In strict nomenclature, the generally accepted design for Canton ware has a bridge in the lower right quarter with no one upon it. In numerous similar variations, figures appear on the bridge, the borders vary, and the landscapes change details.

This plate is part of a group acquired during the nineteenth century by The Mutual Assurance Company in Philadelphia, insurance underwriters. Company records indicate that the dishes were used for dinners which followed the meetings of the Board of Directors. In 1812 the company moved to new offices and bought "one box containing a dining set of China composed of one hundred and seventy-two pieces."[88] Purchases of additional porcelain, some of large sets, were made in 1820, 1825, 1840 and 1893. Presumably these were also Canton, or a related pattern. *(Courtesy: The Mutual Assurance Company)*

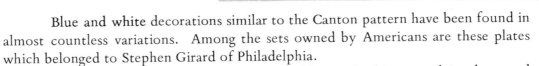

Blue and white decorations similar to the Canton pattern have been found in almost countless variations. Among the sets owned by Americans are these plates which belonged to Stephen Girard of Philadelphia.

It is evident that Girard owned these blue and white porcelain plates and those with his initials (see Monogram section, page 63). He probably sold thousands of other pieces during his years of lucrative trade. In 1816, the *George Washington* listed two boxes of chinaware for Girard in its cargo.[89] Another specific mention of chinaware in the cargo from Canton is made for the *North America* on the 1824–1826 voyage. *(Collection of Girard College, picture courtesy Jonathan Goldstein)*

The two blue and white platters with Chinese landscape decorations were bequeathed by Martha Washington to Nellie Custis Lewis in 1802, and sold to the United States Government in 1878. They are typical of the mid-and-late eighteenth century fragments found during excavations at sites all along America's east coast. They must have been fairly common and plentiful. Top, 16 1/2" by 12 7/8"; bottom, 16" by 13 1/4". *(Courtesy: The Lewis Collection, Smithsonian Institution)*

One of the mass produced decorations on nineteenth century China trade porcelain includes a Chinese landscape with border of alternating "daggers" and "dots." This decoration is called Nanking and can be found in green, or the more usual, blue. These blue Nanking dishes were owned in the family of William Paca (1740–1799) of Maryland. Paca was a lawyer with fine social connections and interest in the political crises of his day. He served on the provincial legislature in Maryland and the First and Second Continental Congresses. He served his state as one of its first Senators, chief Judge and Governor, and was elected to an honorary membership in the Society of the Cincinnati. *(Courtesy: Historic Annapolis)*

Covered, pistol-handled urns of this type can be found with a variety of decorations made for American families. See pages 58, 76 and 150. This example has oval side panels painted with Chinese landscape decorations, detailed gilt and enamel swags, and floral sprays. This urn has a history in the Sargent Bradlee family of Massachusetts. 17" high. *(Courtesy: Benjamin Ginsburg, Antiquarian)*

The sepia and gold Chinese landscape decoration on these fine pistol-handled urns includes a seven-tiered pagoda. The grapevine border decoration around the oval panel can be found also with other American market early nineteenth century decorations such as Commodore Dale's service, p. 204. *(Courtesy: Matthew and Elisabeth Sharpe)*

The pagodas on these dishes may have been inspired by the prominent pagoda at Whampoa Island where European ships anchored while the captains and supercargoes proceeded up the Pearl River twelve miles to Canton to conduct their business. This pagoda was often painted (see illustration) and would have been known to Westerners and Chinese alike. *(Courtesy: Herbert Schiffer Antiques)*

Another pagoda appears on this underglazed blue decorated plate with the four floral groups of the Fitzhugh pattern, and dagger and dot border of the Nanking pattern. This service is believed to have been made for the wedding of Doctor Samuel Cabot and Elizabeth Perkins of Boston in 1812. *(Courtesy: Museum of American China Trade)*

Another view of Whampoa anchorage with the pagoda has been painted on this saucer, perhaps all that remains from what would have been a magnificent tea service. The attention to detail with which Chinese painters copied the scene is a tribute to their sophisticated talent.

Another saucer has been painted with a likeness of the European Hongs at Canton, a scene popular in the West which also was painted both on canvas and porcelain punch bowls. *(Courtesy: Samuel L. Lowe, Jr., Antiques Inc.)*

Oil paintings on Canvas of this sort depict the Hongs at Canton. Such scenes inspired the enamel painted decorations in punch bowls which have become known as Hong bowls. The flags fly before each country's place of business. Paintings of this sort, and therefore the Hong bowls as well, can be dated by known details such as fence lines, trees, further buildings and changes caused by fires. This view dates from about 1820. *(Courtesy: Musuem of American China Trade)*

The decoration on this Hong bowl is painted in polychrome enamels with clarity to the figures and courtyards. Evident in this view are the English, American and French flags. The use of the tricolors for France dates it after the French Revolution. Previous to that, France used a white flag with fleur-de-lis which was not clear to the Chinese painters who painted a blank flag for France. *(Courtesy: The White House)*

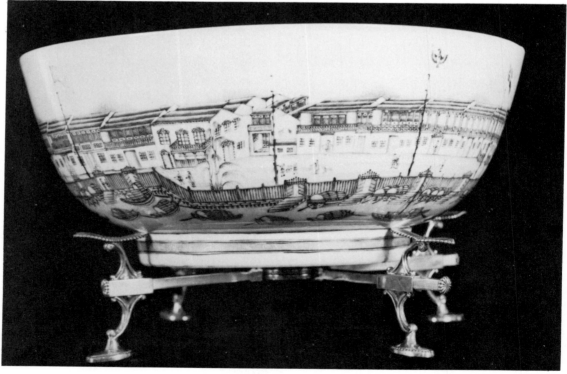

Hong bowls are all rare, probably less than a hundred exist today. Besides the trees and fences, their dating is further facilitated by careful interpretation of the flags and architectural details, for it is known when each country began and ended trade in Canton. This bowl is made further interesting by its painting in black only. 14" diameter. *(anonymous)*

Floral decorations

These fragments of Chinese porcelain plates were excavated in a 1750 context at Front and Pine Streets in Philadelphia. They demonstrate the type of porcelain brought to America through England, until 1784 when America's own ship the *Empress of China* sailed to Canton and initiated direct American trade with China. The variations of patterns using exclusively floral design are numerous. They can be of underglaze blue or overglaze polychrome decoration, or a combination of the two. *(Courtesy: Jon Peter Hineburg)*

These two examples of underglaze blue floral decoration date from the mid-eighteenth century. The plates are typical of imported, mass-market dishes from Canton before the American Revolution period. *(Courtesy: Herbert Schiffer Antiques, Inc.)*

The Chinese Imari decoration of orange, blue and white floral design was made for export from Canton approximately 1740–60. Therefore, this plate was probably sent to Europe and thence to America where it was owned by Paul Revere, Jr. (1735–1818), silversmith of Boston. The plate, 9 1/8" diameter, was part of a dinner service in continuous ownership of the Revere family until pieces were given to the Museum of Fine Arts, Boston, and the Museum of American China Trade.

Paul Revere's interest in political affairs was longstanding by the time he rode from Charlestown to Lexington on April 18, 1775 to warn John Hancock and Samuel Adams that the British were hunting for them, and with two other riders to alert the townspeople of the approaching British troops. Longfellow's poem, "Paul Revere's Ride," immortalized the event. Besides his political affairs, Paul Revere was a creative silversmith, like his father, and also involved with the manufacture of gunpowder, copper bells and cannons. His experience in copper plating, copper plate engraving and hardware manufacture for ships qualified him for his work with Robert Fulton developing copper boilers for steamboats. *(Courtesy: Museum of the American China Trade)*

This piece is part of a very large set of porcelain which descended in several branches of a local Charleston family. *(Courtesy: Charleston Museum)*

The "tobacco leaf" pattern of overglaze polychrome enamels dates from the last decade of the eighteenth century. This service belonged to Ebenezer Stevens of Boston and New York. He was an officer of the Continental Army who took part in the Boston Tea Party before becoming a successful importer in New York. *(Courtesy: Museum of the American China Trade)*

If family tradition can be believed, and in this case extensive research has not been able to confirm or deny the story, Mary Hollingsworth Morris (1776–1820) of Philadelphia made the drawings for the dinner service of which this mug is a part. The simple floral and wheat sprays are said to have been drawn by her about 1800 and carried to Canton by her brother Henry Hollingsworth for duplication on the dinner service. Several pieces of the service remain and they are of diverse forms of a large set.

Henry Hollingsworth sailed for Canton twice as supercargo for Willings and Francis, merchants of Philadelphia.[90] *(Courtesy: Philadelphia Museum of Art)*

Here is a small plate with sprigs of flowers widely spaced. This type of decoration is typical of porcelain found in American homes before the Revolution. This plate is part of a dinner service which has descended in the Jones family of Philadelphia. *(Courtesy: Private Collection)*

The diapered border and sprigged floral decoration of this plate suggest a date circa 1780 for it and the dinner service of which it is a part. This service belonged to Dr. William Eustis of Massachusetts. Eustis had a fascinating career combining medicine and politics, the latter finally dominating his time and establishing his notoriety.

Eustis cared for the wounded at Bunker Hill and eventually served as a hospital surgeon in Boston. Between 1788 and 1794 he sat in the Massachusetts General Court. In 1800 he was elected to Congress for two terms and in 1807 he was appointed Secretary of War, serving during the critical years before the War of 1812. In 1814 he was appointed minister to Holland and served again in Congress from 1820 to 1823. In 1823 and 1824 he was elected governor of Massachusetts. Two other dinner services with Order of the Cincinnati decoration are known to have been owned by William Eustis and were probably made circa 1786.[91] *(Courtesy: The Peabody Museum of Salem)*

Charles Carroll (1737–1832) of "Carrollton" in Maryland, owned the tea service from which this sugar bowl comes. The floral decoration is consistent with the popular late eighteenth century taste in fabrics for small groups of flowers, and the form also suggests this date for the bowl.

Charles Carroll was a farmer and politician who served as a Senator from Maryland between 1789 and 1792. Before he died, he was the last surviving signer of the Declaration of Independence and the wealthiest citizen in the United States. *(Courtesy: John Quentin Feller)*

This border design is found on many American families' services which date from circa 1800 to 1820. The design derives from a European source, probably a pattern book of English or French origin. The background is a warm shade of pinky-brown. *(Courtesy: Matthew and Elisabeth Sharpe)*

This plate is part of a dinner service of simple floral design which descended in a family who lived near Bennington, Vermont during the early part of the nineteenth century. *(Courtesy: The Bennington Museum)*

The family of Henry C. and Mary T. A. Perkins for generations has owned the tea set from which this sugar bowl comes. The porcelain has sacred bird and butterfly decoration in famille rose colors on a celadon background. Usually without monogram or more specific identification, this decoration is one of the standard patterns made for the mass market throughout the nineteenth century. *(Courtesy: The Peabody Museum of Salem)*

The pair of great pitchers with grape decoration are porcelain copies of European silver forms. These have descended in the Cadwalader family of Philadelphia, date from the early nineteenth century and were probably special forms not part of a tea or dinner service. *(Courtesy: Matthew and Elisabeth Sharpe)*

Eighty-seven pieces remain of this dinner service with silver grape vine decoration. The service originally belonged to Benjamin Gratz, a merchant originally from Philadelphia, who lived in Lexington, Kentucky in the first quarter of the nineteenth century. The silver decoration is highly unusual on Chinese porcelain. *(Courtesy: Museum of Early Southern Decorative Arts, Winston-Salem, North Carolina)*

Mauve and gold floral bands encircle the edges of this tureen and platter with central mauve butterfly decoration. The sprightly turn of the butterfly's wing gives movement and depth to the design. This service, which has remained together, was made in the first quarter of the nineteenth century for the Van Rensselaer family of the Albany area of New York. Originally a Dutch patroon family, they branched out during the years and one member, Stephen, founded Rensselaer Polytechnic Institute in Troy, New York in 1824. *(Courtesy: Benjamin Ginsburg, antiquarian)*

The dinner service of which this covered dish is a part, was ordered by Captain Richard Dale (1756–1826) on his last trip to Canton in 1799.[92] The prominent urn decoration with vine border was either a stock design, or was copied later on services such as the following two examples from unknown American families. The Dale service, however, is documented and appears to be the best decorated of this type; therefore, it may be the earliest.

Richard Dale's American naval career is notorious for his service with John Barry and John Paul Jones, as well as numerous distinguished acts in his own command. His trips to Canton under private contract began in 1787 as first mate of the *Alliance,* a vessel purchased by Robert Morris from the United States government. A memento of this trip is the reverse painting on glass of a few members of the crew relaxing with a lady - apparently painted in China under suspicious circumstances for women were clearly not allowed aboard. Nevertheless, another memento of this trip is a punch bowl in the collection of the Philadelphia Maritime Museum with initials "RD" and a painting of a ship similar to the paintings after the *Hall* on Hutchinson's "Treatise on Practical Seamanship" (1777).[93] Dale continued to sail for private parties intermittently until 1799 when he entered the professional United States Navy once more. *(Courtesy: Matthew and Elisabeth Sharpe)*

A variation of the Richard Dale service. *(Courtesy: Daughters of the American Revolution Museum)*

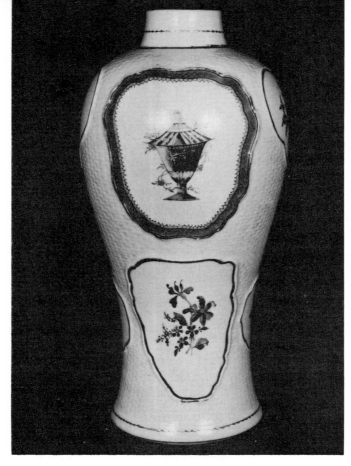

(Courtesy: National Park Service, Norristown, Pa.)

Two pieces of a garniture are decorated with floral border and curtain design below with a basket or urn of flowers. This decoration has been found usually in the Salem area of Massachusetts and can be traced back through the early nineteenth century. *(Courtesy: John Quentin Feller)*

Daniel Webster (1782–1852), lawyer of Salisbury, New Hampshire, owned a blue Fitzhugh dinner service of which this repaired plate is a remnant. Webster had a very successful practice which included his representing New England shipping interests during the conflicts between England and France in the first quarter of the nineteenth century. He was closely involved with the politics of his time, serving in state and national offices including the Senate as Secretary of State. *(Courtesy: Russell Scheider Antiques)*

An orange Fitzhugh dinner service with unusual central floral decoration and wide patterned border around it was owned by members of the Donnell family of Baltimore who owned "Willowbrook" estate. This home was built in 1799 by Thoroughgood Smith, Baltimore's first mayor, and passed into the Donnell family in the next decade. John Donnell, a merchant, married Anna Smith in 1798. An Ann Donnell died in 1839 leaving her husband and a daughter.[94] John S. Donnell died in 1872, aged seventy (a son?).[95] Two rooms from "Willowbrook" are displayed at the Baltimore Museum of Art. *(Courtesy: John Quentin Feller)*

In the period about 1820, Robert Bennett Forbes (1804–1889) acquired and used the dinner service of this decoration. The exciting life of this China trade merchant is extremely important to the development of early nineteenth century Chinese-American commerce. He became a senior factor with Perkins and Company, and later Russell and Company of Boston, two powerful forces of American maritime trade. Among many other accomplishments, he authored *Remarks on China and the China Trade* in 1844. His summer home in Milton, Massachusetts has now become the housing for the Museum of the American China Trade. *(Courtesy: The Peabody Museum of Salem)*

Footnotes

[1] Carl Quellmalz, "Chinese Porcelain excavated from North American Pacific Coast sites," *Oriental Art* 18, No. 2 (Summer, 1972), pp. 148–154.

[2] *Ibid.*

[3] Ivor Noel-Hume, *Pottery and Porcelain in Colonial Williamsburg's Archaeological Collections.* (Williamsburg, Virginia, Colonial Williamsburg Foundation, 1969, pp. 38–43); Jean McClure Mudge, *Chinese Export Porcelain* (Newark, Delaware: University of Delaware Press, 1962, pp. 128–132). On Mexican wares see: David Howard and John Ayers, *China for the West* (London: Sotheby-Parke-Bernet, 1977).

[4] Barbra Liggett, *Archaeology at Franklin's Court.* Harrisburg, Pennsylvania McFarland, 1973: Jonathan Goldstein, "The China Trade from Philadelphia. 1682–1846: A study of Inter-regional Commerce and Cultural Interaction," Ph.D. dissertation, University of Pennsylvania, 1973; Jonathan Goldstein, *Philadelphia and the China Trade, 1682–1846. Commercial, Cultural, and Attitudinal Effects* (University Park and London: Penn State University Press, 1978).

[5] Benjamin Franklin, *The Autobiography of Benjamin Franklin,* edited by Leonard Labaree, Ralph Ketcham, Helene Boatfield and Helene Fineman (New Haven: Yale University Press. 1964, p. 145). Benjamin Franklin to Deborah Franklin, February 19, 1758, in the *Papers of Benjamin Franklin,* edited by Leonard Labaree, VI (New Haven: Yale University Press, 1963), pp. 381. See also letters: Thomas Riche to George Clifford, September 18, 1762; to Q. Hodshon, October 7, 1762, *Riche Letterbooks, 1750–71.* Historical Society of Pennsylvania, Philadelphia (hereafter abbreviated HSP).

[6] For primary source material on the search for northwest route to China see, Thomas Jefferys, *The Great Probability of a Northwest Passage* (London: Thomas Jefferys, 1768). This work contains an appendix entitled: "An Account Labrador Being an Extract from a Journal of a Voyage made from Philadelphia in 1753." The authorship of the "Appendix" has been attributed to Captain Swain of the *Argo* by Harold Eavenson in *Two Early Works on Arctic Exploration* (Pittsburgh: no publisher cited, 1946). See also Berta Solis-Cohen, *Philadelphia's Expeditions to Labrador,* PH 19 (April 1952), 150–62; Edwin Balch, *Arctic Expeditions sent from the American Colonies,* PMHB 31, no. 4 (1970), 419–28; Carl Bridenbaugh, *Cities in Revolt, Urban Life in America* 1743–1776 (New York: Knopf, 1955), p. 202; Bridenbaugh and Bridenbaugh, *Rebels,* p. 329: Goldstein, *Philadelphia and the China Trade,* p. 23.

[7] John Ledyard, *A Journal of Captain Cook's Last Voyage* (Hartford: Nathaniel Patten, 1783); Richard Van Alstyne, *The Rising American Empire* (New York: Oxford University Press, 1960), p. 124; Goldstein, "China" Passim; Goldstein, Philadelphia, p. 26.

[8] By a Yankee, *The Adventures of a Yankee; or the Singular Life of John Ledyard* (Boston: Carter, Hendee, and Babcock, 1831), p. 64; Jared Sparks, *Life of John Ledyard, the American Traveller* (Boston: Charles C. Little and James Brown, 1847), p. 175; Samuel Shaw, *The Journals of Major Samuel Shaw. The First American Consul at Canton,* edited by Josiah Quincy (Boston: Wm. Crosby and H. P. Nichols, 1847), p. 133; Clarence Ver Steeg, "Financing and Outfitting the First United States Ship to China," PHR 22 (February 1953), 5–6; Goldstein, "China" Passim; Goldstein, *Philadelphia,* p. 26.

[9] Samuel Shaw (Canton) to John Jay, January, 1789, in *Journal of Major Shaw,* edited by Josiah Quincy, (Boston: 1847), pp. 350–351.

[10] Primary source material on the *Empress'* 1784 voyage to China includes: Shaw, *Journals;* the "Receipt Book, F. Molineux for Account of Captain Green," Canton, 1784 and 1786, University of Pennsylvania Library Rare Book Collection, Philadelphia; and the "John Green Papers," property of the Thibault family, Saint David's, Pennsylvania. The Molineux item is an account kept on the first Empress voyage (Canton, 1784) and on the second voyage (Canton, 1786). The Green papers consist of miscellaneous *Empress* material, including the ship's manifest from its first China voyage. HSP owns a Chinese watercolor painting of the vessel in Chinese waters. The painting is part of a mother-of-pearl Chinese fan. Secondary material on the first voyage includes Versteeg, "Financing," and William Fairburn, *Merchant Sail,* I (Center Lovell, Maine:

Fairburn Marine Educational Foundation, 1945–55), pp. 497–98. See also Robert Morris to John Jay, November 27, 1783, in *The Correspondance and Public Papers of John Jay,* edited by Henry Johnston, III, (New York, Putnam 1891), p. 97; Goldstein, "China" Passim; Goldstein, Philadelphia, p. 27.

[11]Robert Peabody, *Log of the Grand Turks,* p. 79.

[12]Ann Wite, "The Hong Merchants of Canton," unpublished Ph.D. dissertation, University of Pennsylvania, 1968, pp. 36–82; Hosea Morse, *The Chronicles of the East India Company Trading to China, 1635–1834,* V (Oxford: Oxford University Press, 1926), pp. 56–93; W. E. Cheong, "Trade and Finance in China, 1784–1834. A Reappraisal." *Business History* (Liverpool) 7, no. 1 (January, 1965), pp. 34–38. The name *Kung-hang* is pronounced the same in both Mandarin and Cantonese. It is sometimes confused with *Kuan-hang* (Cantonese), which also means a government *hang* or company, but is a general term for such organizations. The members of the cohong were called *Kuan-shang,* "official merchants." Goldstein, "China," Passim; Goldstein, *Philadelphia,* pp. 27–29.

[13]Letters, Samuel Shaw to Winthrop Sargeant, November 19, 1785, Society Miscellaneous Collection, HSP; Thomas Randall to Alexander Hamilton, August 14, 1791, in *The Industrial and Commercial Correspondence to Alexander Hamilton,* edited by Arthur Cole (Chicago; A. W. Shaw Company, 1928), p. 132; Goldstein, "China," *Passim;* Goldstein, *Philadelphia,* p. 30.

[14]*Massachusetts Centinel* (Boston), May 18, 1785. The following newspapers also carried information about the *Empress'* successful completion of its first voyage: *Daily Advertiser* (New York), May 16, 1785; *New York Packet,* May 16, 1785; *Providence Gazette,* May 18, 1785; *Newport Mercury,* May 21, 1785; *Freeman's Journal* (Philadelphia), June 22, 1785; *Delaware Gazette* (Wilmington), January 18, 1786; Goldstein, "China," *Passim;* Goldstein, *Philadelphia,* p. 31.

[15]*Pennsylvania Packet* (Philadelphia), May 16, 1785; Goldstein, "China," *Passim;* Goldstein, *Philadelphia, p. 31.*

[16]South Carolina's tariff is given in the *Providence Gazette,* May 29, 1784. Pennsylvania's is mentioned by Fitzsimmons in a speech on the tariff, April 18, 1789, in Thomas Hart Benton's *Abridgment* (1857–1861), pp. 41–42; *The Public Statutes at Large of the United States of America,* I, p. 25; Kenneth Scott Latourette, *History of Early Relations Between the United States and China* (New Haven, 1917), p. 78; Tyler Dennett, *Americans in Eastern Asia* (New York, 1941), p. 8.

[17]On diplomatic conditions in the Orient and West Indies, see letter, Parish and Company to Stephen Girard, Philadelphia, Pennsylvania, on microfilm in American Philosophical Society Library, Philadelphia; all correspondence to or from Girard will be understood to have come from this collection, unless otherwise indicated. "Stephen Girard" hereafter abbreviated as "S. G." Samuel Bemis, *Jay's Treaty* (New Haven: Yale University Press, 1962), pp. 469–71; Holden Furber, "The Beginnings of American Trade with India," *New England Quarterly* (June 1938), pp. 240–65; Albert Gares, "Stephen Girard's West India Trade, 1789–1812," unpublished edited dissertation, Temple University, 1947, pp. 72–88; Samuel Bemis, *A Diplomatic History of the United States* (New York: Holt, 1951, pp. 100–102). Goldstein "China Trade," Passim; A piece of John Jay's porcelain appears in this book. Goldstein, *Philadelphia,* passim.

[18]Helen Augur, *Passage to Glory,* (Garden City, New York, 1946), p. 141.

[19]Samuel W. Woodhouse, "Log and Journal of the ship *United States* on a voyage to China in 1784," *Pennsylvania Magazine of History and Biography,* LV (1931), p. 230.

[20]Abraham Ritter, *Philadelphia and her Merchants as Constituted Fifty to Seventy Years Ago,* (Philadelphia, 1860), p. 181; Sydney Greenbie, "Stephen Girard–Mariner and Merchant (of the China Trade), *Asia,* XXV (December, 1925), p. 1058; Kenneth Scott Latourette, *The History of Early Relations between the United States and China 1784–1844,* pp. 69–70.

[21]Agnes Danforth Hewes, *Two Oceans to Canton. The Story of the Old China Trade.* (New York, 1944), p. 64.

[22]Statistics were taken at Canton, from the records of the American consulate. Stateside figures were inaccurate, since many American ships cleared American ports destined for China but never got there while many cleared destined for other ports, yet wound up in Canton. Robert Waln, Jr., "Abstracts of Philadelphia Trade to Canton"; "Memo Book, Canton, September 1819 to January 1820," p. 52. Papers, Library Company of Philadelphia; Jeremiah Reynolds, *Voyage of the United States Frigate Potomac* (New York: Harper, 1835), p. 380.

[23]SG to Richard Parish, March 29, 1817; Robert Waln, Sr., entry for April 19, 1819, Letterbook, 1815–19, WP; Invoice, August 1, 1822, Latimer Papers, Library of Congress; Michael Greenberg, *British Trade and the Opening of China, 1800–1842* (Cambridge: Cambridge University Press, 1951), pp. 153–58. Thomas Truxton to David Lewis, December 19, 1818, Miscellaneous Manuscript Collection, New York Historical Society; John McMaster, *The Life and Times of Stephen Girard,* I (Philadelphia: Lippincott, 1918), pp. 303–4;

Biography of Stephen Girard (Philadelphia: Thomas C. Bonsal, 1832), p. 95; [Stephen J. Winslow], *Biographies of Successful Philadelphia Merchants* (Philadelphia: James K. Simon, 1864), pp. 181–85; Joan Thill, "A Delawarean in the Celestial Empire," (unpublished M. A. thesis, University of Delaware, 1973), pp. 262–63; Harold Gillingham, *Marine Insurance in Philadelphia, 1721–1800,* (Philadelphia: privately printed, 1933), p. 100; *Desilver's Philadelphia Directory,* (Philadelphia, 1830), p. 9; *M'Elroy's Philadelphia Directory,* (Philadelphia: Orrin Rogers, 1841), p. 12; 1842 edition, pp. 12, 326; Goldstein, *Philadelphia,* passim.

[24]On the problem of glutting, see also: Timothy Pitkin, *A Statistical View of the Commerce of the United States,* (New Haven: Durrie & Peck, 1835), p. 304; Letters: William A. Foster to Richard Ashurst, March 20, 1827, HSP, Unger Collection; Joseph Archer to Jabez Jenkins, November 10, 1833, HSP; Shaw, *Journals,* pp. 350–51.

[25]For a description of British trade, see Letter: Forester & Company to SG, November 22, 1822; David Owen, *British Opium Policy in China and India* (New Haven: Yale University Press, 1934).

[26]Robert Bennet Forbes, *Personal Reminiscences* (Boston: Little, Brown, 1878), p. 174; Daniel Henderson, *Yankee Ships in China Seas* (New York: Hastings House, 1946), p. 161; Goldstein, *Philadelphia,* p. 49.

[27]Letter: John Latimer to Henry Latimer, April 3, 1829. John R. Latimer Papers, University of Delaware Library, Newark; Goldstein, *Philadelphia,* p. 50.

[28]John Latimer to Joseph Lesley, June 23, 1847, Latimer Papers, University of Delaware; Carol Ranshaw, "Calendar of the University of Delaware Collection of the John Latimer China Trade Papers," unpublished Master's thesis, School of Library Science, Drexel Institute of Technology, 1953, p. 23; Goldstein, *Philadelphia,* p. 51; Goldstein, "China", passim.

[29]Letter: Benjamin Wilcocks to John Latimer, April 26, 1829, Latimer Papers, Library of Congress, Goldstein, *Philadelphia,* p. 51.

[30]Charles Stelle, "American Trade in Opium to China Prior to 1820," PHR (December 1940), 429; Kimball, *The East India Trade,* p. 17; Goldstein, *Philadelphia,* p. 52.

[31]Jacques M. Downs, "American Merchants," *Bus. Hist. Rev.,* XLII (Winter, 1968), p. 421; Charles C. Stelle, "American Opium," *Pac. Hist. Rev.,* IX (December, 1940), p. 430.

[32]United States Congress, Senate, *Message of the President (on) Commerce and Navigation in the Turkish Dominions,* S. Doc. 200, 25th Cong., 3d sess., 1839, pp. 81–86; Jacques Downs, "American Merchants and the China Opium Trade, 1800–1840," *Business History Review* 42 (Winter, 1968), 421: Stelle, "Trade," pp. 430–41. Letter: SG to Mahlon Hutchinson and Myles McLeveen, January 2, 1806; Goldstein, *Philadelphia,* pp. 53–54; Goldstein, "China," passim.

[33]Letters: Woodmas and Offley to SG, September 27, 1815; Dutilh & Company to SG, March 24, 1819; Benjamin Seebohm, *Memoirs of the Life and Gospel Labors of Stephen Grellet,* II (London: A. W. Bennett, 1860), p. 28; [John Stephens], *Incidents of Travel in Greece, Turkey, Russia and Poland,* I (New York: Harper, 1838), p. 189; David Finnie, *Pioneers East* (Cambridge: Harvard University Press, 1967), p. 29; Walter Wright, "American Relations with Turkey to 1831," (unpublished Ph.D. dissertation, Princeton University, 1928), p. 67; Goldstein, *Philadelphia,* p. 54.

[34]Hosea Morse, *The International Relations of the Chinese Empire,* I (London: Longmans, Green, 1910), pp. 201–11; Morse, "The Provision of Funds for the East India Company's Trade," *Journal of the Royal Asiatic Society,* Part II (April, 1922), p. 227; Letters, George Blight to SG, March 4, November 21, 1807; Charles Macfarlane, *Constantinople in 1828* (London: Saunders and Otley, 1829), p. 33; Wright, "Relations," p. 53; Stelle, "Prior to 1820," 432–33; Goldstein, *Philadelphia,* p. 54.

[35]George Cooke, *China* (London: G. Routledge, 1858), p. 179. United States Congress, Senate, *Dispatches from Ministers to China,* letter, William Reed to Secretary of State Cass, June 30, 1858, S. Ex. Doc. 30, 36th Cong., 1st sess., p. 357. John Fairbank, "The Legalization of the Opium Trade Before the Treaties of 1858," *The Chinese Social and Political Science Review,* 17 (July, 1933), 215–63; Owen, British Opium, 265; Goldstein, *Philadelphia,* p. 68.

[36]On domestic manufacture, see: Graham Hood, *Bonnin and Morris of Philadelphia: The First American Porcelain Factory, 1220–1222* (Chapel Hill: University of North Carolina Press, 1922); John Watson, *Annals of Philadelphia and Pennsylvania,* II (Philadelphia: Carey & Hart, 1844), p. 272.

[37]John R. Latimer, lists of American vessels with records of destinations, imports, exports, Canton, 1828–34. Joseph Downs Memorial Manuscript Collection, Winterthur Museum, Winterthur, Delaware; Tyler Dennett, *Americans in Eastern Asia* (New York: Macmillan, 1922), p. 8; Mudge, *Chinese,* pp. 16, 124–25; Dulles, *Old China,* p. 211.

[38]Now open to the public under the auspices of the National Trust for Historic Preservation.

[39]Chew family papers preserved at Cliveden, property of The National Trust for Historic Preservation in Philadelphia.

[40]David S. Howard and John Ayers, *China for the West,* Vol. II. London: Sotheby-Parke-Bernet, p. 486, plate 499.

[41]Two hundred and fifty-eight pieces are at the Metropolitan Museum of Art, four pieces are at the Maryland Historical Society, and four pieces are in a dealer-collector's collection.

[42]David S. Howard, *Chinese Armorial Porcelain,* p. 426.

[43]George Earlie Shankle, *State Names, Flags, Seals, Songs, Birds, Flowers and Other Symbols,* New York. the H. W. Wilson Company, 1976, p. 205.

[44]Shankle, p. 195.

[45]Shankle, p. 194.

[46]Shankle, p. 192.

[47]Howard, p. 678.

[48]Nathaniel H. Morgan, *A History of James Morgan...and his Descendants,* (Hartford, 1869), pp. 92–93; Clare Le Corbeiller, "China Trade Armorial Porcelain in America," *Antiques,* December, 1977, pp. 1124–1129.

[49]Le Corbeiller, "China Trade," *Antiques,* December, 1977, p. 1125.

[50]*Dictionary of American Biography,* VIII, pp. 368–369.

[51]Frances Follin Jones, curator of Collections, The Art Museum, Princeton University, letter of June 14, 1979.

[52]Jane Gaston Mahler, Charleston, South Carolina, letter of March 15, 1980 and related documents of the Manigault family.

[53]Jane Gaston Mahler, Charleston, South Carolina, letter of March 15, 1980 and related documents of the Manigault family.

[54]Goldstein, "Girard," p. 33.

[55]*An Exhibition of China Trade Porcelain,* New Haven, Connecticut: New Haven Colony Historical Society, 1968, p. 23.

[56]*Winterthur Newsletter,* Volume XXX, Number 5, September, 1979.

[57]Mudge, p. 157

[58]Howard, p. 77.

[59]Jonathan Goldstein, *Philadelphia and the China Trade, 1682–1846,* University Park and London, The Pennsylvania State University Press, 1978, p. 17.

[60]For example, the Rose Medallion round central decoration, Mount Vernon decoration, landscapes in round panels, portraits in round or oval decorations.

[61]Washington Papers, Washington to Varick, January 1, 1784.

[62]Homer Eaton Keyes, "The Cincinnati and Their Porcelain," *The Magazine ANTIQUES,* February, 1930.

[63]Ibid.

[64]Ibid.

[65]Mudge, p. 172.

[66]*University Hospital Antique Show, 1972 catalog,* p. 162, number 19.

[67]Mudge, pages 186 and 224.

[68]Peters, *Currier and Ives,* plate 180.

[69]George W. Cullum, "The Struggle for the Hudson," *Narrative and Critical History of America,* VI, J. Winsor, ed., pp. 317–318.

[70]Cullum, "Struggle," *Narrative,* VI, pp. 350 and 352.

[71]James Biddle, "Joseph Bonaparte," *Pennsylvania Magazine,* Volume 55, p. 212.

[72]Patricia C. Fleming, "A Toddy Jug with Philadelphia Connections," *University Hospital Antiques Show Catalog,* 1972, pp. 186–188; Joseph Downs, "A Chinese Lowestoft Toddy Jar," *Bulletin of The Metropolitan Museum of Art,* XXX, 2 (February 1935), pp. 39 and 40.

[73]Ibid.

[74]Alice Morse Earle, *China Collecting in America,* 1892.

[75]Stephen Decatur, "The Commodore Decatur Punchbowl," *The Magazine ANTIQUES,* April, 1932.

[76]Charles G. Dorman, "Captain Richard Dale at Canton," *Catalog of the University Hospital Antiques Show,* 1972, p. 179.

[77]Ibid.

[78]"The Commodore Decatur Punchbowl," *Antiques,* XXXII, December, 1937, pp. 296—7.

[79]Robert E. Peabody, *The Log of the Grand Turks,* 1926, pp. 93 and 94.

[80]"An Exhibition of China Trade Porcelain," The New Haven Colony Historical Society, 1968, p. 23, number 4.

[81]Mudge, p. 71.

[82]Mudge, p. 84; Elinor Gordon, ed., *Chinese Export Porcelain, Antiques* magazine, pages 129 and 167.

[83]*Winterthur Newsletter,* February 21, 1957 from information supplied by James Foster, Director of the Maryland Historical Society.

[84]Mudge, p. 193.

[85]The traditional story of the Quaker and cow story is this: Mary Hollingsworth made a drawing for this porcelain and gave it to her brother Henry Hollingsworth who was a supercargo from Philadelphia. In Canton, the porcelain was decorated in sepia with this Quaker and cow design. Mary gave the set to her husband, Israel Morris, who felt the gold rim band was too worldly for his taste. Therefore, the sepia and gold set was kept in the Hollingsworth family, and on the next trip to Canton a set decorated in black was made, and this set was accepted by Morris.

[86]Lloyd E. Hawes, M.D., "Benjamin Waterhouse, M.D.," *Boston Medical Library,* Studies I, 1974, pp. 36—39.

[87]Ibid, p. 43.

[88]Anthony N. B. Garvan and Carol A. Wojtowicz, *Catalog of The Green Tree Collection,* The Mutual Assurance Company, 1977, p. 103.

[89]Goldstein, *Girard,* p. 33.

[90]Philadelphia: *Three Centuries of American Art,* pp. 214, 215; "Hollingsworth Book," family papers of Dr. John B. Carson, Newtown Square, Pennsylvania.

[91]See pages 134 and 135.

[92]Charles G. Dorman, *University Hospital Antique Show catalog,* 1972, Philadelphia, pp. 178—181.

[93]See page 154.

[94]*Baltimore Sun,* April 30, 1839.

[95]Marian Buckley Cox, *Donnells of Willowbrook,* privately published.

Bibliography

Manuscript Sources

Estate of Stephen Girard, dec'd, Philadelphia. Stephen Girard Papers (on microfilm in American Philosophical Society Library, Philadelphia).

Henry Francis duPont Winterthur Museum. Winterthur, Delaware. Joseph Downs Memorial Manuscript Collection.

Historical Society of Pennsylvania, Philadelphia. Unger Collection

"John Green Papers." Thibault family, Saint David's, Pennsylvania.

Library of Congress. Latimer Papers.

New York Historical Society. Miscellaneous Manuscript Collection.

"Receipt Book, F. Molineux for Account of Captain Green." Canton: 1784 and 1786. University of Pennsylvania Library Rare Book Collection, Philadelphia.

University of Delaware Library, Newark. John R. Latimer Papers.

Waln, Robert, Jr. "Abstracts of Philadelphia Trade to Canton." Papers, Library Company of Philadelphia.

Waln, Robert, Jr. "Memo Book, Canton. September 1819 to January 1820." Papers, Library Company of Philadelphia.

Published Sources

An Exhibition of China Trade Porcelain, designed to illustrate the wares imported to the Port of New Haven. New Haven, Connecticut: The New Haven Colony Historical Society, 1968.

Augur, Helen. Passage to Glory: John Ledyard's America. Garden City, New York: Doubleday, 1946.

Balch, Edwin. "Arctic Expeditions sent from the American Colonies," Pennsylvania Magazine of History and Biography, 31, no. 4, 1970.

Beers, Burton F. China in Old Photographs 1860–1910. New York: Charles Scribner's Sons, 1978.

Bemis, Samuel. A Diplomatic History of the United States. New York: Henry Holt, 1951.

Bemis, Samuel. Jay's Treaty. New Haven, Connecticut: Yale University Press, 1962.

Beurdeley, Michel. Chinese Trade Porcelain. Rutland, Vermont: Charles E. Tuttle and Co., 1962.

Biddle, Edward. "Joseph Bonaparte, as recorded in the Private Journal of Nicholas Biddle," Pennsylvania Magazine of History and Biography, vol. 55. Philadelphia: Historical Society of Pennsylvania, 1931.

Bridenbaugh, Carl. Cities in Revolt, Urban Life in America 1743–1776. New York: Knopf, 1955.

By a Yankee. The Adventures of a Yankee; or the Singular Life of John Ledgard. Boston: Carter, Hendel and Babcock, 1831.

Cheong, W. E. "Trade and Finance in China, 1784–1834. A Reappraisal." Business History (Liverpool) 7, no. 1 (January 1965).

Chou, Calvin. The Hollow Line in Dating Chinese Porcelains. San Francisco: Chinese Art Appraisers Association, 1978.

Cole, Arthur, ed. The Industrial and Commercial Correspondence to Alexander Hamilton. Chicago: A. W. Shaw Co., 1928.

Cooke, George. China. London: G. Routeledge, 1858.

Cox, Marian Buckley. Donnels of Willowbrook. Privately published, no date.

Crossman, Carl L. Chinese Export Paintings, Furniture, Silver and Other Objects, 1785 to 1865. Salem: Peabody Museum, 1970.

Crossman, Carl L. A Design Catalog of Chinese Export Porcelain. Salem: Peabody Museum, 1964.

Crossman, Carl L. The China Trade. Princeton: The Pyne Press, 1972.

Cullum, Gorge W. "The Struggle for the Hudson," Narrative and Critical History of America. Cambridge: Houghton, Mifflin and Co., The Riverside Press, 1888.

Decatur, Stephen. "The Commodore Decatur Punchbowl," The Magazine ANTIQUES. April, 1932.

Dennett, Tyler. Americans in Eastern Asia. New York: Macmillan, 1922.

Desilver's Philadelphia Directory. Philadelphia, 1930.

Dorman, Charles G. "Captain Richard Dale at Canton," University of Pennsylvania Hospital Antiques Show Catalog. 1972.

Downing, A. J. A Treatise on the Theory and Practice of Landscape Gardening. New York and London: Willy and Putnam, 1841.

Downs, Jacques M. "American Merchants," *Business History Review* XLII (Winter 1968).

Downs, Joseph. "A Chinese Lowestoft Toddy Jar," *Bulletin of the Metropolitan Museum of Art* XXX, 2 (February 1935).

Dulles, Foster Rhea. *China and America.* Princeton, New Jersey: Princeton University Press, 1946.

Earle, Alice Morse. *China Collecting in America.* 1892.

Eavenson, Harold. *Two Early Works on Arctic Exploration.* Pittsburgh: no publisher cited, 1946.

Fairbank, John. "The Legalization of the Opium Trade Before the Treaties of 1858," *Chinese Social and Political Science Review* 17 (July 1933).

Fairburn, William. *Merchant Sail,* I. Center Lovell, Maine: Fairburn Marine Educational Foundation, 1945–1955.

Finnie, David. *Pioneers East.* Cambridge: University Press, 1967.

Fleming, Patricia C. "A Toddy Jar with Philadelphia Connections," *University Hospital Antiques Show Catalog.* Philadelphia: 1972.

Forbes, Robert Bennett. *Personal Reminiscences.* Little, Brown, Boston, 1878.

Franklin, Benjamin. *The Autobiography of Benjamin Franklin.* Edited by Leonard Labaree, Ralph Ketcham, Helene Boatfield and Helene Fineman. New Haven, Connecticut: Yale University Press, 1964.

Furber, Holden. "The Beginnings of American Trade with India," *New England Quarterly.* (June 1938).

Gares, Albert. "Stephen Girard's West India Trade, 1789–1812." Unpublished edited dissertation. Temple University, 1947.

Garvan, Anthony N. B. and Carol A. Wojtowicz. *Catalogue of The Green Tree Collection.* Philadelphia: The Mutual Assurance Co., 1977.

Gates, Edith. "The Washington China," *Quotarian* X, 2 (February 1932).

Gillingham, Harold. *Marine Insurance in Philadelphia, 1721–1800.* Philadelphia: privately printed, 1933.

Goldstein, Jonathan. *Philadelphia and the China Trade 1682–1846; Commercial, Cultural and Attitudinal Effects.* University Park and London: Pennsylvania State University Press, 1978.

Goldstein, Jonathan. "The China Trade from Philadelphia, 1682–1846: A Study of Inter-regional Commerce and Cultural Interaction." Ph.D. dissertation, University of Pennsylvania, 1973.

Gordon, Elinor, ed. *Chinese Export Porcelain.* New York: Main Street/Universe Books, 1975.

Greenberg, Michael. *British Trade and the Opening of China, 1800–1842.* Cambridge: Cambridge University Press, 1951.

Greenbie, Sydney. "Stephen Girard - Mariner and Merchant (of the China Trade)," *Asia* XXV, (December 1925).

Hawes, Lloyd E., M.D. "Benjamin Waterhouse, M.D.," *Boston Medical Library.* Studies I, 1974.

Henderson, Daniel. *Yankee Ships in China Seas.* New York: Hastings House, 1946.

Hewes, Agnes Danforth. *Two Oceans to Canton. The Story of the Old China Trade.* New York: 1944.

"Hollingsworth Book." Family papers of Dr. John B. Carson, Newtown Square, Pennsylvania.

Hood, Graham. *Bonnin and Morris of Philadelphia: The First American Porcelain Factory, 1770–1772.* Chapel Hill: University of North Carolina Press, 1972.

Howard, David Sanctuary. *Chinese Armorial Porcelain.* London: Farber and Farber Limited, 1974.

Howard, David Sanctuary and John Ayers. *China for the West.* London: Sotheby-Parke-Bernet, 1977.

Humelsine, Carlisle H. "Vision and Revision at the Governor's Palace: Fresh Findings suggest new Considerations," *Colonial Williamsburg Today* I, 3 (Spring 1979).

Hyde, J. A. Lloyd. "The Menagerie," *University Hospital Antiques Show Catalog.* 1978.

Jefferys, Thomas. *The Great Probability of a Northwest Passage.* London: Thomas Jefferys, 1768.

Johnston, Henry, III, ed. *The Correspondance and Public Papers of John Jay.* New York: Putnam, 1891.

Keyes, Homer Eaton. "The Cincinnati and their Porcelain," *The Magazine ANTIQUES.* (February 1930).

Kimball, Gertrude. *The East-India Trade of Providence from 1787 to 1807.* Providence: Preston and Rounds, 1896.

Latourette, Kenneth Scott. *History of Relations Between the United States and China.* New Haven: 1917.

Le Corbeiller, Clare. "China Trade Armorial Porcelain in America," *The Magazine ANTIQUES.* (December 1977).

Le Corbeiller, Clare. "Oriental Menagerie," *University of Pennsylvania Hospital Antiques Show Catalog.* Philadelphia: 1978.

Ledyard, John. *A Journal of Captain Cook's Last Voyage.* Hartford: Nathaniel Patten, 1783.

Liggett, Barbara. *Archaeology at Franklin's Court.* Harrisburg: McFarland, 1973.

Los Angeles County Museum Bulletin of the Art Division. Vol. 7, no. 1 (Winter 1955).

MacFarlane, Charles. *Constantinople in 1828.* London: Saunders and Otley, 1829.

McMaster, John. *The Life and Times of Stephen Girard.* 2 vols. Philadelphia: Lippincott, 1918.

Malone, G. Damas, ed. *Dictionary of American Bibliography.* New York: Charles Scribner's Sons, 1928–1936.

M'Elroy's Philadelphia Directory. Philadelphia: Orrin Rogers, 1841.

Morgan, Nathaniel H. *A History of James Morgan...and his Descendants.* Hartford: 1869.

Morison, Samuel Eliot and Henry Steele Commager. *The Growth of the American Republic.* 2 vols. New York: Oxford University Press, 1940.

Morse, Hosea. *The Chronicles of the East India Company Trading to China, 1635–1834.* Oxford: Oxford University Press, 1926.

Morse, Hosea. *The International Relations of the Chinese Empire,* I. London: Longmans, Green, 1910.

Morse, Hosea. "The Provision of Funds for the East India Company's Trade," *Journal of the Royal Asiatic Society.* Part II (April 1922).

Mount Vernon China. Mount Vernon: The Mount Vernon Ladies' Association of the Union, 1962.

Mudge, Jean McClure. *Chinese Export Porcelain for the American Trade.* Newark: University of Delaware Press, 1962.

Noel-Hume, Ivor. *Pottery and Porcelain in Colonial Williamsburg's Archaeological Collections.* Williamsburg: Colonial Williamsburg Foundation, 1969.

"Old-Time New England," *Bulletin of the Society for the Preservation of New England Antiquities.* Vol. LI, no. 2. Boston: Fall 1960.

Owen, David. *British Opium Policy in China and India.* New Haven, Connecticut: Yale University Press, 1934.

Palmer, Arlene M. *A Winterthur Guide to Chinese Export Porcelain.* A Winterthur Book/Rutledge Books. Crown Publishers, Inc., 1976.

Parke-Bernet Galleries, Inc. *English and Chinese Porcelain.* New York: Parke-Bernet Galleries, Inc., October 29, 1971.

Peabody, Robert E. *The Log of the Grand Turks.* Boston and New York: Houghton Mifflin Co., The Riverside Press, Cambridge, 1926.

Perkins, Bruce Coleman. "Chinese Export Porcelain for the Reeves Collection of Washington and Lee University," *Washington Antiques Show Catalog.* 1978.

Philadelphia, Three Centuries of American Art. Philadelphia: Philadelphia Museum of Art, 1976.

Pitkin, Timothy. *A Statistical View of the Commerce of the United States.* New Haven, Connecticut: Durrie and Peck, 1835.

Pleasants, Henry. *Thomas Mason, Adventurer.* Philadelphia: The John C. Winston Co., 1934.

Peters, Harry T. *Currier and Ives, Printmakers to the American People.* Garden City: Doubleday, Doran and Co., Inc., 1942.

Paine, Ralph D. *Ships and Sailors of Old Salem.* Chicago: A. C. McClurg and Co., 1912.

Phillips, James Duncan. *Salem in the Eighteenth Century.* Boston and New York: Houghton Mifflin Co., The Riverside Press, Cambridge, 1937.

Phillips, James Duncan. *Salem in the Seventeenth Century.* Boston and New York: Houghton Mifflin Co., The Riverside Press, Cambridge, 1933.

Phillips, John Goldsmith. *China-Trade Porcelain.* Cambridge: Harvard University Press, 1956.

Quellmalz, Carl. "Chinese Porcelain Excavated from North American Pacific Coast Sites," *Oriental Art,* 18, no. 2 (Summer 1972).

Quincy, Jonah, ed. *The Journals of Major Samuel Shaw: The American Consul at Canton with a Life of the Author.* Boston: William Crosby and H. P. Nichols, 1847.

Ranshaw, Carol. "Calendar of the University of Delaware Collection of the John Latimer China Trade Papers." Unpublished Master's Thesis. School of Library Science. Drexel Institute of Technology, 1953.

Reynolds, Jeremiah. *Voyage of the United States Frigate Potomac.* New York: Harper, 1835.

Reynolds, Valrae, Phillip H. Curtis and Yen Fen Pei. *2000 Years of Chinese Ceramics.* Newark, New Jersey: The Newark Museum, 1977.

Richardson, E. P. *Painting in America from 1502 to the Present.* New York: Thomas Y. Crowell

Ritter, Abraham. *Philadelphia and Her Merchants as Constituted Fifty to Seventy Years Ago.* Philadelphia: Published by the author, 1860.

216

Scharf, J. Thomas and Thompson Westcott. *History of Philadelphia, 1609–1884.* 3 vols. Philadelphia: L. H. Everts and Co., 1884.

Schiffer, Herbert, Peter and Nancy. *Chinese Export Porcelain.* Exton, Pennsylvania: Schiffer Publishing Limited, 1975.

Seebohm, Benjamin. *Memoirs of the Life and Gospel Labors of Stephen Grellet,* II. London: A. W. Bennett, 1860.

Shankle, George Earlie, Ph.D. *State Names, Flags, Seals, Songs, Birds, Flowers and Other Symbols.* Republished 1976. New York: The H. W. Wilson Co., after 1934 and 1938 copyrights.

Simpson, Stephen. *Biography of Stephen Girard.* Philadelphia: Thomas C. Bonsal, 1832.

Solis-Cohen, Berta. "Philadelphia's Expeditions to Labrador." *Pennsylvania History* 19 (April 1952).

Sparks, Jared. *Life of John Ledyard, the American Traveller.* Boston: Charles C. Little and James Brown, 1847.

Stelle, Charles. "American Trade in Opium to China Prior to 1820," *Pacific History Review* IX (December 1940).

Stephens, John. *Incidents of Travel in Greece, Turkey, Russia and Poland,* I. New York: Harper, 1838.

Thill, Joan. "A Delawarean in the Celestial Empire." Unpublished M. A. Thesis, University of Delaware, 1973.

Tudor-Craig, Sir Algernon. *Armorial Porcelain of the Eighteenth Century.* London: The Century House, 1925.

United States Congress. Senate. *Dispatches from Ministers to China.* Letter, William Reed to Secretary of State Cass, June 30, 1858. S. Ex. Doc. 30, 36th Cong., 1st sess., p. 357.

United States Congress. Senate. *Message of the President [on] Commerce and Navigation in the Turkish Dominions.* S. Doc. 200, 25th Cong., 3rd sess., 1839.

Van Alstyne, Richard. *The Rising American Empire.* New York: Oxford University Press, 1960.

Ver Steeg, Clarence. "Financing and Outfitting the First United States Ship to China," *The Pacific Historical Review* 22 (February 1953).

Watson, John. *Annals of Philadelphia and Pennsylvania,* II. Philadelphia: Carey and Hart, 1844.

Whitehead, James W. "The Reeves Collection of Chinese Export Porcelain of Washington and Lee University," *Washington Antiques Show Catalog,* 1978.

Whitehill, Walter Muir. *The East India Marine Society and the Peabody Museum of Salem, a Sesquicentinnial History.* Salem: Peabody Museum, 1949.

Whitehill, Walter Muir. *George Crownshield's Yacht Cleopatra's Barge, and a Catalog of the Francis B. Crowninshield Gallery.* Salem: Peabody Museum, 1959.

Whitehill, Walter Muir [intro. by]. *Portraits of Shipmasters and Merchants in the Peabody Museum.* Salem: Peabody Museum, 1939.

[Winslow, Stephen J.] *Biographies of Successful Philadelphia Merchants.* Philadelphia: James K. Simon, 1864.

Winsor, Justin. "The Portraits of Washington," *Narrative and Critical History of America.* Vol. VII, p. 563. Boston and New York: Houghton, Mifflin and Co., The Riverside Press, Cambridge, 1888.

Winterthur Newsletter. February 21, 1957.

Winterthur Newsletter, XXX, no. 5 (September 1979).

Wite, Ann. "The Hong Merchants of Canton." Unpublished Ph.D. dissertation, University of Pennsylvania, 1968.

Woodhouse, Samuel W. *The Voyage of the Empress of China.* Vol. LXIII. Philadelphia: The Historical Society of Pennsylvania, 1939.

Woodhouse, Jr., M.D., Samuel W. "Log and Journal of the Ship *United States* on a Voyage to China in 1784." *Pennsylvania Magazine of History and Biography.* Vol. 55, p. 225–258. Philadelphia: Historical Society of Pennsylvania, 1931.

Wright, Walter. "American Relations with Turkey in 1831." Unpublished Ph.D. dissertation, Princeton University, 1928.

Zieber, Eugene. *Heraldry in America.* Department of Heraldry. Philadelphia: The Bailey, Banks and Biddle Co., 1895.

Index

A, 89
ABL, 103
ABW, 36
Adams, Abigail, 67, 107
Adams, John, 67, 107
Adams, Samuel, 145, 196
Albany, New York, 9, 203
Alexander, arms, 53
  Major-General William, 53
Allen, William, 9
Allenson's, Rev. Francis Academy, 66
Alliance, 14, 154, 204
AME, 137
American Antiquarian Society, 91
American-Asiatic trade, 12
American Indian figure, 61
American Indians, 7
American Philosophic Society, 19
American Revolution, 47, 62, 77, 195
Ammen, Daniel, 83
Amory, John, 62
Amory, Thomas, 62
Amoy, 23
Amsterdam, 10
Anchor, 112, 113
Anderson, Deborah Fairfax, 59
Anglo-French hostilities, 12
Annapolis, Maryland, 34
Aphrodisiac, 10
Arab, 92
Argo, 9
Armorial decorations, 31–58
Arms of Liberty, 143
Asia, 14
AST, 68
Atahualpa, 36
Atlantic Insurance Company, 14
Atlantic Ocean trade, 9
A Treatise on Practical Seamanship, 153, 154
Axes, 36

B

BA, 118
Bache family, 176
Bahama Islands, 31
Baltimore, 10, 14, 19, 65, 67, 70, 73, 88, 150, 157, 207
Baltimore *Advertiser,* 133
Baltimore Museum of Art, 207
Bamboo, 11
Bancker, Charles N., 14
Bancker, James A., 14
Bank of New Haven, 98
Barataria, 84
Barry, John, 154, 204
Batavia, 18, 52
BCW, 151
Beech family, 92
Bells, 196

Bennington, Vermont, 47, 200
Bennington Works, 24
BEV, 70
Biddle family, 108
Billings, 153
Bingham, 19
Birch, William, 37, 38, 168–170
Bird and sacred flower, 104
Black decoration, 194
Blights, 19
Boilers, 196
Bombay, 52
Bonaparte, Charles Joseph, 88
Bonaparte, Elizabeth Patterson, 88
Bonaparte family, 150
Bonaparte, Jerome, 88, 150
Bonaparte, Joseph, 150
Bonaparte, Napoleon, 88, 150
Bonnin and Morris, 24
Bonnin and Morris China Manufactory, 8
Bordentown, New Jersey, 150
Boston, 10, 12, 14, 19, 22, 34, 36, 50, 57, 62, 69, 72, 77, 133, 134, 156, 182, 183, 192, 196, 197, 199, 208
Boston Tea Party, 197
Boudinot, Elias IV, 51, 76
Boudinot, Hannah Stockton, 76
Boudinot, Susan Vergereau, 76
Bowles, Ralph Bart, 131
Boxer, 163
Boyden, Dwight, 182
Bradford, William, 76
Bradley, 82
Brandywine, 53
Britain, 12, 15, 16, 19
British East India Company, 8, 10, 16, 17
British Levant Company, 18, 19
British ships, 11
Brown, John, 45, 111
Brown, Joseph, 111
Brown, Moses, 111
Brown, Nicholas, 111
Bryant, John, 36
BSP, 118
Bunker Hill, 47, 199
Burgoyne, John, 148
Butterfly, 105

C

C, 89, 103
Cabot, Doctor Samuel, 192
Cabbage, 105
Cadwalader family, 108
Calcutta, 52
California, 7
Cambridge, Massachusetts, 32, 174
Canal, 94
Canals, 37
Cannons, 196

Canton, 9, 11, 14, 28, 30
Canton pattern, 22, 103, 186, 187
Cape Horn, 9
Cape of Good Hope, 9, 10, 52
Capitol, 144
Caribbean Sea trade, 9
Caroline, 36
Carpenter, 48
Carroll, Charles, 199
"Carrollton," 199
Carter, Mary Walker, 84
Catesby, Mary Walker Carter, 84
CB, 76
Celadon, 201
Centennial of 1876, 145
CFCS, 60
Charles, II, 33
Charleston, South Carolina, 8, 56, 60, 61, 62, 197
Charlestown, Massachusetts, 134, 196
Chase, Jeremiah Townley, 35
Chase, Richard, 35
Chesapeake Bay, 157
Chester County, Pennsylvania, 66
Chevrons, 36
Chew, Benjamin, 25
Chew family, 24, 27, 28, 103
Chew, Mrs. Benjamin, 25, 30
"China Cottage," 22
China fever, 12
Chinaware, 186
Chinese Customs Service, 16
Chinese landscape decorations, 181–194
Chinese watercolor paintings, 181
Chippendale, Thomas, 34
Cincinnatus, Lucius Quinctius, 130, 131
Cinnamon, 11
CJB, 88
Clark, Fort, 90
Classical figures, 103
Clayton, S., 56
Clements coat of arms, 54
Clements family, 54
Clinton, DeWitt, 94
Clinton, Maria Franklin, 94
Cliveden, 24, 27, 28, 30, 103
CMJ, 84
Coffee, 52, 184
Cohong, 10, 11, 15
Colby, John A., 43
Colden, Lieutenant Governor, 58
Color plates, 93–108
Columbia, 14
Combe Martin, Devon, 32
Committee of Safety, 65]
Concord, New Hampshire, 43
Connecticut, 78
Constitution, 70
Constitution, 125

Constitution, U.S., 12
Continental Army, 50, 130, 132
Continental Congress, 51, 55, 66, 78
Continental Navy, 130
Cook, Captain James, 9
Cooke, W., 167
Cope, Thomas Pym, 14
Copper plating, 196
Coramandel Coast, 14
Cotting family, 89
Cotton, 111
Cotton fabric, 11
Country traders, 16
Cow, 172
Cows, 174, 176
Cowpox vaccination, 174
Cox, Benjamin, 126
Cox, Edward, 126
Crary, Elizabeth Denison, 79
Crary, Peter, 79
Cuban, 184
Cumberland, 90
Cupid, 59
Currier and Ives, 144, 145, 148
Currier, Nicholas, 145, 148
Custis family, 85
Custis, George Washington Parke, 95
Customs Service, 11
CVD, 73

D

Dale, Commodore, 124, 190
Dale, Richard, 154, 204, 205
Decatur, Commodore Stephen, Sr., 152
Decatur family, 152
Decatur, Stephen, 84, 152
Declaration of Independence, 44, 66, 68, 78, 121, 144–149, 199
DeGartoux, Father Jean DuHall, 15
Delaware, 64, 72
Delaware, 152
Delaware River, 33
Denmark, 22
Dent and Company, 16
Derby, Elias Haskett, 12, 52, 59, 154
Derby family, 59
Derby, J., 59
Desdemona, 13, 19
Dewey, Commodore Matthew, 182
DFA, 59
Dispatch, 167
DL, 127
Donnell, Ann, 73
Donnell family, 207
Donnell, John, 73, 207
Donnell, John S., 207
"Don't give up the ship," 163
Doolittle, Amos, 136
Downing, A. J., 23
Dragon, 104
Drake's Bay, 7
Dressing Box, 11

Druggist, 69
Duane family, 173
Duane, James, 58
Duane, Mary Alexander Livingston, 58
Duane, W. L., 173
Duer, William, 9
Dunmore, Lord, 31, 58
Dunn, Nathan, 22
Dutch, 9
Dutilh and Company, 19
Dutilh, Edward, 19
DWMC, 94

E

Eagle, 44, 93, 97, 99, 100, 101, 103, 109–136, 145, 147, 165
Eagle Decoration
  Type I, 111
  Type II, 114
  Type III, 115
  Type IV, 116
  Type V, 117
  Type VI, 118
  Type VII, 119
  Type VIII, 119
  Type IX, 120
  Type X, 121
  Type XI, 123
  Type XII, 125
  Type XIII, 127
  Type XIV, 128
  Type XV, 129
EAL, 60
East India Company, 32
East Indian Marine Society, 70
EAT, 86
Eckfeldt, Adam, 137
Eckford, Henry, 165
Edwin, David, 151
EF, 74
EHM, 92
Eight Immortals, 105
Eight regulations, 11
EJ, 92
Empress of China, 10, 11, 12, 14, 24, 48, 96, 97, 133, 134, 154, 195
Empress of China bowl, 11
England, 9, 22
English porcelain, 129
Engraving, 171
Engraving, copper plate, 196

Erie Canal, 94
ET, 151
Eustis, William, 134, 135
Eustis, Dr. William, 199
Eutaw, 19
"Excelsior," 40
Experiment, 14
EY, 75

F

Falkland Islands, 156

Fame, 103, 127, 133, 134, 135
Famille rose, 182
Fan, 12
Fan, with Empress of China, 12
Fans, 22
Fans, lacquered, 11
Farmington, Connecticut, 92
Feller, John Quentin, 92
Fermor, Lady Julia, 33
First New Haven National Bank, 98
First Treaty Settlement, 24
Fisher, Mary Livinia, 64
Fisher, Rodney, 64
Fishing, 176
Fishing scene, 171
Fitzhugh 28, 30, 54, 55, 56, 57, 61, 63, 73, 82, 84, 85, 86, 99, 103, 108, 118, 119, 170, 192, 207
Flag, 165
Flags, 129, 153, 193, 194
Floral decorations, 195–208
Floral design, 129
Foochow, 23
Forbes, Robert Bennett, 16, 17, 208
Fowle, Daniel Gould, 185
France, 22, 62, 130, 131, 150, 193
Francis, John, 45
Franklin, Benjamin, 8, 9, 62, 65, 145
Franklin Insurance Company, 14
Freeman, Constant, 102, 134
Fremont House, 182
French and Indian War, 47
French Island, 77
French porcelain, 129
French Revolution, 193
Frenchtown, Maryland, 157
Friendship, 156
Front Street, 195
Fulton, Robert, 196
Funerary urn, 93
Fungmanhi, 37
Fur, 14
Fur trade, 9
Furs, 10

G

G, 72
Garniture, 46
Gates, Horatio, 148
General Washington, 14
General Washington Resigning his Commission, 144
George Washington, 45, 112, 187
German porcelain, 129
Germantown, 30, 53
GHM, 61
Gibbs, Jabez, 161
Gibson, James, 65
Ginseng, 9, 10, 11, 15, 17, 63
Girard, Stephen, 12, 13, 14, 19, 63, 187
Gloucester, Massachusetts, 50
Gloves, 11

219

Goat, 172, 173
Gold, 14
Goldsborough, Charles, 55
Goldsborough family, 55
Goldsborough, Louis Malesherbes, 55
Goldsborough, Robert, 55
Gore, Christopher, 72
Gore, Frances Pinckney, 72
Gore, John, 72
Grand Turk, 14, 154
Grand Turk bowl, 11
Grant, Ulysses Simpson, 83, 184
Grapevine border, 54, 67, 121, 122, 141, 190, 201, 202, 204
Gratz, Benjamin, 202
Great Britain, 96
Green, Captain John, 10, 11
Green, John, 10, 154
Green, Nathaniel, 142, 156
GS, 87
Guerriere, 70
Gunpowder, 62, 196

H

H, 70, 85
Haldeman, Jacob W., 22
Hall, 97, 153, 154, 157, 204
Hallowell, Sarah, 34
Hamilton, Alexander, 130
Hancock, John, 32, 145, 196
Hancock, Nathaniel, 32
Handcock, 32
Handkerchiefs, 22
Happiness symbol, 184
Hardware, 196
Harriet, 10
Hartford, Connecticut, 9, 48
Harvard University, 72, 174
Hatteras, Fort, 90
Hawaiian Islands, 23
HCS, 69
Heard, 24
HEJ, 176
Hemphill, William, 72
Henly, Robert, 85
Henry Smith punch bowl, 112
Herrera, Gonzalo Jose de, Conde of Fernandina, 184
Herrera, Gonzalo Luis, Marquis de Villalta, 184
Herrera, Marquis de Almendares Ignacio, 184
Hinam joss house, 11
Hingham, Massachusetts, 134
Hiram Lodge, Order of Freemasons, 104, 142
Holker, John, 9
Holland, 22
Hollingsworth family, 172, 173
Hollingsworth, Henry, 198
Holmes, Rebecca, 62
Hong bowl, 193, 194
Hong Kong, 23, 24
Hong merchants, 10, 154
Hongs, 192—194

Hooper, Robert, 81
Hope, 14
Hope, 45, 52, 92, 112, 113, 121
Houckgeest, Andreas E. Van Braam, 95
HS, 112, 113
Hudson River, 10, 94, 130
Hull, Isaac, 70, 84, 125
Humpton, Richard, 135, 136
Hunt family, 78
Huntington, Samuel, 78
Hutchinson, William A., 153, 154, 204

IG, 161
IH, 125
Illinois, 44
Imari, 196
Imperial Court, 10
In God We Hope, 45, 121
Independence Hall, 145
India, 15, 16, 19, 22, 64
India China, 186
Indian Ocean, 52
Indians, 7, 9
Indigo, 22
Insurance companies, 14
Insurance Company of North America, 14
Insurance Company of Pennsylvania, 14
Insurance underwriters, 186
Ireland, 62
Isle of France, 52

J

J, 93
JA, 62
JAA, 67
Jackson, Mary, 65
JAD, 73
Jardine, 24
Jardine, Matheson and Company, 16
Jay, 14
Jay, John, 10, 96, 121
Jay's Treaty, 12, 96
JB, 141
JCR, 86
JD, 59
Jefferson, Thomas, 62, 72, 93, 145
Jenner, Dr. Edward, 174
JES, 124
JG, 65
JHRH, 117
JJ, 96
JLH, 99
JM, 92
Jones family, 198
Jones, Hanna Elizabeth, 176
Jones, Isaac Cooper, 176
Jones, John Paul, 204
Jones, Mary Hemphill, 72
Jones, Morgan, 72

Jones, Thomas Ap Catesby, 84
Justice, 40
JWP, 82

Kaolin, 8
Knirsch, O., 148
Knox, Henry, 10, 130, 133, 134
Kuang-hang, 10

Labrador, 9
Lake Champlain, 85
Lake Erie, 94
Landscape decorations, Chinese, 181—194, Western, 167—180
Latimer, John, 14, 16, 17
Lead, 10
Ledyard, John, 9, 14
Lee coat of arms, 57
Lee family, 57, 103
Lee, Henry (Light Horse Harry), 57, 134
Lee, Robert E., 57
Leedom family, 86
Leedom, Jonathan, 86
Leeds pottery, 63
L'Enfant, Major Pierre Charles, 131
Lettsom, Dr. John, 174
Lewis, J., 93
Lewis, Joseph Saunders, 176
Lewis, Mordecai, 14
Lewis, Nellie Custis, 188
Lexington, Kentucky, 202
Lexington, Massachusetts, 196
Liberty, 40
Lincoln, Benjamin, 134
Linguist, 11
Liverpool, 153
Liverpool jugs, 151
Livingston, 145
Livingston family, 60
Livingston Manor, 58
Livingston, Robert, 58
London, 10, 174
Londonderry, New Hampshire, 47
Longfellow, Henry W., 196
Louisburg, Canada, 8

M

M, 100, 118
Macao, 151, 154
MacDonald, arms, 53
Made in China, 185
Manchester, Massachusetts, 36, 74
Mandarin, 28, 30, 91, 106, 182, 183, 184
Manigault, Charles Izard, 56, 61
Manigault coat of arms, 56
Manigault, Gabriel Henry, 56, 61
Manila, 52
Mansfield, Lord, 143

Marblehead, Massachusetts, 81
Marine decoration, 153–166
Marine Society, 36
Marine view, 166
Maryland, 55, 199
Maryland Historical Society, 67
Mason, Thomas, 62
Masonic emblems, 104, 137–142
Massachusetts, 72, 199
Massachusetts Centinel, 12
Massachusetts Historical Society, 36
Mayor of New York City, 58
McKean, Thomas, 66
McVicar and Company, 64
Memento, 69
Mexican War, 84
Mexico, 7
MH, 72
Milton, Massachusetts, 208
Minerva, 59
Ming Dynasty, 7
Miniature tea service, 74, 171, 176
Minton (porcelain), 57
Mississippi, 85
Mississippi Territory, 50
Missouri, 20, 22
MLRF, 64
Monogram, 28, 30
Monogrammed decorations, 59–92
Montesquieu, 13, 19
Monticello, 93
Morgan, Daniel, 148
Morgan, Elias, 49
Morgan, John, 48, 49
Morris family, 108, 171, 172, 173
Morris, Mary Hollingsworth, 173, 198
Morris, Robert, 9, 10, 11, 12, 14 65, 154, 204
Morton bowl, 37, 38, 39
Morton, General Jacob, 37
Mount Holly, New Jersey, 22, 63
Mount Vernon, 37, 103, 133, 168–170
Munson, Major William, 142
Murray, William, 143
Museum of the American China Trade, 196, 208
MW, 95

N

Nankeen, 7, 11, 156
Nanking, city, 23
Nanking pattern, 116, 189, 192
Nantucket, Massachusetts, 87
Napoleon, 88
Narcotic, 15, 16
Nassau Hall, 51
National Trust for Historic Preservation, 30
Naval architect, 165
Navigation Act, 8, 9
NEA, 127
Nelson, Thomas, 68
Neptune, 68, 156
New Castle, Delaware, 66, 157

New Hampshire, 43
New Haven Colony Historical Society, 92, 142
New Haven, Connecticut, 14, 68, 78, 82, 98, 104, 156
New Jersey, 18
New Jersey, 46, 53
New Jersey State Museum, 154
New London, Pennsylvania, 66
New South Wales, 56
New Windsor Cantonment, 130
New York, 9, 10, 11, 14, 24, 37, 47, 50, 53, 58, 60, 77, 79, 83, 94, 96, 133, 134, 145, 148, 154, 156, 173, 197
"New York from Brooklyn, 1803," 38
New York harbor, 37
New York, royal colony, 31
New York Society of the Cincinnati, 132
New York State coat of arms, 40, 41, 42
Newark, New Jersey, 73
Newton, Massachusetts, 70
Nicholas Brown and Company, 111
Nixon and Walker, 65
Nixon, John, 65
Norfolk, Virginia, 84
North America, 187
North Carolina, 185
Northwest Passage, 9
Notman, John, 23

O

Observations on the Cowpox, 174
Offley, David, 19
Ohio, 50
Old Ironsides, 125
Olyphant, 24
Opium, 15–20
Order of the Cincinnati, 57, 102, 130–136
Oriental clothing, 147
OS, 69
Ostend, 22

P

Paca, William, 189
Pacific Squadron, 84
Pagoda, 190–192
Painting, reverse on glass, 204
Paintings, Chinese watercolor, 181
Pallas, 14, 133, 134
Paper borders, 11
Parker, Catherine Van Dyke, 73
Parker, Daniel, 9, 154
Parkyns, George I., 167
Pascaqoula, 24
Pattern book, 54, 128, 200

Patterson, Elizabeth, 88, 150
"Paul Revere's Ride," 196
Pavot Somnifere, 16
Peabody, Joseph, 12, 156
Peabody Museum of Salem, 154, 181
Peacock, 182
Peale, Charles Willson, 166
Peale, James, 166
Peale, Raphaelle, 166
Peale, Rembrandt, 166
Peale, Rubens, 166
Peale, Titian, 166
Pearl River, 191
PEC, 79
Penn family, 33
Penn, Hannah, 33
Penn, John, 33
Penn, Thomas, 33
Penn, William, 33
Penn's Landing, 8
Pennsylvania, 18
Pennsylvania, 33, 43, 135
Pennsylvania Hospital, 167
Pennsylvania Packet, 12
Pennsylvania Railroad, 157
People's Republic of China, 24
Pepper, 52
Perine, David M., 67
Perkins and Company, 208
Perkins, Elizabeth, 192
Perkins, Henry C., 201
Perkins, J. and T. H., 18
Perkins, Mary T. A., 201
Philadelphia, 8, 9, 10, 12, 14, 17, 18, 19, 20, 22, 24, 25, 30, 51, 53, 54, 62, 63, 64, 70, 71, 76, 79, 86, 95, 103, 108, 115, 145, 151, 152, 154, 157, 167, 171, 176, 186, 187, 195, 198, 201, 202
Philadelphia Maritime Museum, 154, 204
Philadelphia Mint, 137
Phillips, William, 79
Phoenix Insurance Company, 14
Pine Street, 167, 195
Pingree, David and Ann, 63
Pinqua, 154
P.M., 43
Point Breeze, 150
Political decorations, 143–152
Pomfret, Earl of, 33
Pondicherry, Acheen, 14
Porcelain, 11, 17, 20, 25
Porcelain, English, 57
Port Seatrain, 24
Portugal, 22
Portuguese ships, 11
Princeton, New Jersey, 47
Princeton University, 51

Providence, Rhode Island, 14, 45, 111, 112
Prussia, 22
Puqua, 11

Quaker, 111, 172
Quaker and cow, 172, 173
Quincy, Massachusetts, 67, 107

R

R, 86
Railroad car, 157
Railroads, 23, 184
Raleigh, 43
Ralston, Ashabel, 14
Randall, Thomas, 77, 11, 14
Rangoon, 52
RCC, 142
RCH, 81
RD, 154, 204
Read and Gray, 22
Redwood, William, Jr., 167
Remarks on China and the China Trade, 208
Rensellaer Polytechnic Institute, 203
RES, 74
Revere family, 196
Revere, Paul Jr., 196]
Reverse painting on glass, 204
Revolution, 130, 148
Rhode Island, 45
Rhode Island Abolition Society, 111
Rice, 10
Rickman, Lieutenant John, 9
Rockland Mansion, 176
Roger's Rangers, 47
Roman Senate, 130
Roosevelt, Theodore, 88
Rose Canton, 105
Rose Medallion, 28, 30, 83, 88, 89, 90, 103, 185
Rotunda, 144
Rousseau, 13, 19
Rum, 9, 62
Russell, 24
Russell and Company, 208
Russia, 11

S

Saint Memin, 152
Saint Petersburg, 52
Salem, Massachusetts, 14, 52, 59, 70, 82, 89, 126, 154, 156, 206
Salisbury, New Hampshire, 207
Sally, 63
San Francisco, 7, 23, 24
Saratoga, New York, 148
Sargent family, 50
Sargent, Ignatius, 50

Sargent, Winthrop, 50
Sassoon, 24
SB, 82, 183
Schuyler, Philip J., 148
Schuylkill River, 176
Scotland, 31
Seal of the United States, 37, 109, 111, 112, 113, 114
Seal of New York City, 37
Sears family, 77
Sears, Isaac, 77
Seymour, Samuel, 37, 38, 168–170
SGW, 83
SH, 78
Shanghai, 23, 24[
Shanghai Steam Navigation Company, 24
Shaw, Samuel, 10, 14, 77, 133, 154
Sherman, 145
Shipley family, 69
Shirts, 22
Shipbuilding, 62, 165
Shopmen, 16
Shringham, Silas, H., 90
SHS, 90
Silk, 7, 20, 156
Silk window blinds, 11
Silver, 14, 16
Silver decoration, 202
Silver forms, 201
Silversmith, 196
Sisom, Priscilla, 62
Smallpox, 174
Smith, Anna, 207
Smith, Elizabeth Clifford, 71
Smith, Henry, 45, 112
Smith, Oliver, 69
Smith Point, 36
Smith, R., 85
Smith, Thomas W., 71
Smith, Thoroughgood, 207
Smugglers, 16, 17
Smuggling, 16
Smyrna, Turkey, 18, 19
Society Hill, 8
Society of Friends, 111
Society of the Cincinnati, 17, 103, 130–136, 189
    badge, 130, 131
Spain, 22
Spero, 52
Spices, 18, 52
SS, 133, 168
Stage coach, 157
Stark, John, 47
Steamboat, 157, 196
Sterling, Earldom, 53

Sterling, Lord, 53
Stevens, Ebenezer, 197
Stewart, William, 18
Still life painting, 166
"Still Life with Strawberries," 166
Stockbridge, Massachusetts, 10
Stockton, Hannah, 76
Stoke Park, Buckinghamshire, 33
Stoneware, 8
Strong, Allen B., 46
Stuart, Gilbert, 151
Sturgis, Elisabeth Perkins, 74
Sturgis, Russell, 36, 74
Sturgis, William, 36
Sugar, 18, 22, 184
Sultan of Turkey, 165
Sumatra, 156
Sun, 47
Supercargo, 133
Surrender of Burgoyne at Saratoga, 44, 144, 148, 149
Surrender of Cornwallis at Yorktown, 144
SW, 83
Swain, Gideon, 87
Sweden, 22
Swift, Charles, 96
Swift, John White, 96
Swift, Mary, 96, 97
Sword, John D. and Company, 24
Sylph, 19
Synchong, 37

T

T, 91
Tariff policy, 12
Tea, 7, 10, 11, 17, 18, 20, 22, 24, 31, 156, 181
Tea, bohea, 11
Tea, gunpowder, 11
Tea, hyson, 11
    hyson skin, 11
Tea, souchong, 11
Tea tariff, 12
Textile mill, 184
Thayer, Colonel Sylvanus, 121
The Grand Turk, 52, 59
The Magazine ANTIQUES, 152
The Mutual Assurance Company, 186
Thomas, Isaiah, 91
Thompson, Edward, 64
Thompson, George, 176
Thomson, Ann Renshaw, 86
Thomson, Charles, 11

222

Thomson, Edward, 86
Thread, 22
Ticonderoga, New York, 148
Tilghman, Colonel Tench, 133
Tilghman, Edward, 151
Tilghman, Tench, 134
TM, 62
TN, 68
Tobacco leaf pattern, 197
Tomb, 93
Tortoise shell combs, 22
Townley, Lady Margaret, 35
Townsend, Amos, 68
Townsend, Dr. David S., 134
Townsend, Ebenezer, 68
Townsend, Sarah Howe, 68
Treatise on Practical Seamanship, 204
Trenton, New Jersey, 47, 75
Trident, 24
Trieste, 22
Troy, New York, 203
Trumbull, John, 121, 144, 145, 148
Trumpet, 121
Truxton, 14
TSS, 77
Tucker, William Ellis, 24
Turkey, 19
Turkish opium, 17
Turpentine, 62

U

Ulster County, Ireland, 47
Union Line, 157
United States, 12, 163
United States Department of State, 121
United States government, 12
United States Military Academy, 121
United States Mint, 51
United States Supreme Court, 51
USG, 83

V

Valley Forge, 53
Van Dyke, Catherine Vanderpool, 73
Van Dyke, James, 73
Van Rensselaer family, 203
Van Rensselaer, Stephen, 203
Vanderford, Benjamin E., 70
Vans, W. Jr., 154

Varick punch bowl, 132
Varick, Richard, 132
Vaughn, Samuel, 34
Vermont, 24
VH, 78
Virginia, 8, 31, 57, 68, 84, 85, 103, 134, 168

W

W, 57, 174
Wagner, Tobias, 14
Wagner family, 19
Wall paper, 11
Waln, Robert, Jr., 22, 23
Waln, William, 18, 19
War of 1812, 125, 162, 163, 199
Washington, George, 85, 93, 103, 108, 130, 132, 133, 134, 136, 148, 151, 168
Washington, George, Farewell Address, 151
Washington, Martha, 95, 136, 188
Washington, Mary Ball, 108
Washington's Birthday, 10
Watercolor paintings, Chinese, 181
Waterhouse, Dr. Benjamin, 174
WC, 163
Webster, Daniel, 207
Wedgwood, 128
Weeping willow tree, 93
West, Benjamin, 167
West, Captain E., 154
West Indian trade, 12
West Indies, 52, 62, 63
West Point, New York, 121
Western landscape, 46
Western landscape decorations, 167–180
Wetherburn Tavern, 8
Wetmore and Company, 24
Whampoa Island, 191, 192
Wharton, Charles, 14
Wharton, Thomas I., 14
Wheat, 47
Wheat sprays, 198
Wheatland, Stephen G., 83
Whitall, John, 18
White Clay Creek, 8
White, Joseph Page, 82
White House, 83
Wilcocks, Benjamin Chew, 16, 18, 19, 25, 151
Wilcocks, James, 18, 19
Wilcocks, R. H., 18
Wilkes and Liberty bowl, 143

Wilkes, John, 143
Williamsburg, Virginia, 8, 31
Willing and Francis, 19, 198
Willing and Morris, 19
"Willowbrook," 207
Window blinds, 11
Winterthur collection, 45
Winterthur Museum, 67, 92, 118, 181

Winthrop family, 57
WLD, 173
Woodmas and Offley, 19
Woolen cloth, 10
Worcester, Massachusetts, 91

Yam Shinqua, 43
Yard, Edward, 75
Yard goods, 11, 22, 181